A Newbies Guide to Developing an iPhone Game App

Minute Help Guides

Minute Help Press
www.minutehelp.com

Table of Contents

Part I: How to get inside the walled garden – the Apple way, or no way

How to develop an app for the iPhone – an overview

Please read this! Don't skip ahead just yet.

There are many people who can benefit from this guide. This introduction to creating iPhone game apps will guide the absolute beginner through the steps needed, and by the end you will have a finished app that you can run on your iPhone, iPad or iPod touch.

Even if you have some experience as a programmer, you can use this guide to learn about Apple's technologies and design theories. These are key aspects of what is sometimes referred to as Apple's "ecosystem."

There are several reasons for the spectacular success of Apple technologies over recent years, and part of that has to do with the fact that Apple enjoys a unique position in the technology industry. As a leading maker of software, operating systems and the hardware that runs them, Apple exercises strong control over the "look and feel" of the software you create.

As a leading vendor of software that people buy for their Apple devices, they also have considerable influence over the technologies you'll use to develop your app. If Apple feels your app can create problems for the iPhone user, or interfere with the functions of the iPhone, they will not approve your app for the App Store and their millions of users may never even see it.

You may have heard that Apple co-founder Steve Jobs values control, and that's right.

Developing an app for your iPhone involves two major steps and this guide walks you through both. We show you how to deal with Apple – get the tools you need to develop software, register as an Apple Developer, get your iPhone prepared to run your code and how to install your programs onto your iPhone.

We also show you all the technology you need to know to develop game apps (and many other types of apps, as well). Get Apple's Xcode – a great suite of software applications that makes software development easier. Learn Objective-C – the programming language almost all Apple developers use. See the user interface elements that help you capture that look and feel that Apple customers crave and see how you can turn these elements into games you create.

Also, please keep in mind that these instructions aren't just for the iPhone. Apple's iOS operating system also runs iPads and iPod touches, so this information will apply to these devices too.

What you need to use this book

We don't assume you have any previous programming experience. We start with some very basic overviews to familiarize you with some common concepts and terms. Then we show you how to use them, hands on, to create your own iPhone game app. In the process, you'll learn a lot more, and you'll discover how the skills you've gained can be applied to bigger, more complex projects. But there are some minimum requirements.

You need a Mac – Apple makes the iPhone. Apple makes the iOS operating system that runs on it. Apple makes Xcode, the most important tool for creating software for the iPhone. And Apple makes the Mac. You'll need to, ideally, own the most modern Mac you can afford. If you have to get by on a Mac you just have regular access to (a friend sets up an account for you on their machine, or you have access at your school), you will need administrative access to install some of the necessary software. Contact your IT department for school or work computers.

You'll need a Mac that can run Mac OS 10.5 (Leopard), 10.6 (Snow Leopard) or the newly released OS 10.7 (Lion) to run up-to-date development tools.

You need to be "computer savvy." We assume you have never programmed. That's fine, and welcome! But you do need to know right-click from left-click, that menu items have keyboard shortcuts (like Command-C for "Copy,"), how to select items, drag them, what interface elements are (buttons, scrollbars, tabs, menus), and so on. If you don't know how to use computers pretty well, you may need to re-think your grand ambitions until you do.

You need $99. We're not going to lie to you, the only way for a beginner to get their app onto an iPhone is to work closely with Apple. You're going to have to register as an iOS Developer, and that carries an annual fee of $99. Don't let that discourage you, though. Apple currently sells copies of its Xcode software to any Mac user for only $4.99. You'll be able to get all the tools you need to get started, including a cool iPhone simulator that allows you to get your code working without risking a lot of money. You can register when you have your code working, but sooner or later, you'll need to do this.

NOTE: If you're a student, you may be eligible to join Apple's iOS Developer and Mac Developer for little or nothing. It will only last while you're in school so enjoy it while you can! Check at Apple's Developer website (http://developer.apple.com/) for more information.

You need an iPhone – Honestly, this also falls into the "sooner or later" category. As we just mentioned, you can test using the iOS simulator for a while, but before you submit your app to the app store, you'll have to test it on the real deal. If you have an iPad instead that will work as well. You can find a relatively new, used iPod touch very inexpensively, which will give you most of the same features without a monthly phone contract – if you have convenient Wi-Fi access. Besides, you'll want to get as familiar as possible with the way apps work while you make them.

Humor and patience – There's the Hollywood movie cliché, where the master hacker plugs into the bad guy's computer system and in minutes has the secret plans, and has seized control of his security system. That's not how it works. There's a certain amount of experimenting, which means trial-and-error, which can be frustrating. Problem-solvers and puzzle-solvers do well at programming. Try to enjoy the challenges. Keep on learning and having fun!

What this book will teach you

This is not a book about creating apps without programming. Any game worth making will require some custom code. We're going to show you just how much code Apple already provides and how to use that to your advantage. Then we'll show you how that code goes together – the code Apple creates for you. Next we show you how to write custom code to add new features. We teach you how the Objective-C programming language works, so you can create your own custom code. We'll finish by showing you where to find more information and keep increasing your skills.

Some helpful tips on using this book

To make this book easier to read, we're going to use a few, easy-to-remember conventions. We'll always capitalize names of parts of the user interface when you're using software. For instance, all the menus are capitalized, like File. If we want you to go to your File menu and choose Save (for instance), we'll just write File > Save. Names of toolbar icons, text fields, and so forth, will all be capitalized.

Also, when the computer outputs a message to you, we'll use a very computer-y looking font, like this – "Error: Expected ":" token, before ")" – (sounds like something a computer would say, doesn't it?). Later, when we're looking at code examples straight out of Xcode, if you're reading on a color screen you'll see the words have several different colors. This is a feature Xcode offers – it helps you keep track of different operations in you software code, by color-coding certain keywords. We'll talk more about keywords later.

Usually, if we **boldface** something, it's a note, warning, a section title or something else important that we want to call to your attention. *Italics* will often indicate some specific technical term, especially if it's the first time we've used it.

Finally, there may be places where you have to choose a name to use in your code. Sometimes, convention suggests that you use the name of your project. For instance, we're going to start by creating a project called Hello World. You'll find that Xcode will create files with names like Hello_WorldAppDelegate or Hello_WorldViewController. Occasionally, we'll express that concept by using some generic phrase like YourName or YourFile.

It'll be helpful to have your copy of Xcode open so you can follow along with the examples as we work with them. Try to type the code in, instead of copying the code. We'll look at Xcode's auto-completion feature and see how it makes typing quick and easy.

You'll need to create a few graphics during the course of these examples. You don't need to be any kind of artist to create these (you'll see ours, and they're pretty crude). If you're totally graphics-challenged, we have tips on easy ways to make your own. You can always search for images online, of course, but we recommend that you only use photos that are legally in the public domain. You may want to check sites like Wikimedia, Creative Commons and Internet Archive for a start. Don't leave your great idea vulnerable to lawsuits over using someone else's content!

The big question: Will this book tell me how to make the super-cool game that's in my head?

Like most of life, the answer is yes and no. Even a beginner can make a pretty cool iPhone game, but you'd probably need pretty exact instructions and that's a problem – we don't know what game is in your head, because it's still in your head, see?

If you follow the tutorials in this book, you'll end up with a couple of simple games that you create from scratch and you can run on your iPhone (the code has all been tested on actual devices). But you'll also finish with a tremendous knowledge about all the technology that goes into creating an iPhone game app, and how you can use it to help you get at that idea in your head. You'll also learn easy ways to find out more about how to master these skills.

If you're willing to take the time, you can learn how to make that game you've dreamed of making. Enjoy!

How to register as an Apple Developer

Most of you are not ready to make this step yet, although you all soon will be. However, we want to keep this in mind during all the steps we take. We want to produce our application according to good programming practices – especially practices approved by Apple.

If you aren't ready yet to invest that sum in the project, don't worry. Although Xcode is free to all Apple Developers, anyone can purchase it from Apple's Mac App Store for only $4.99. The software includes an iOS simulator that you can use to run and test your software until you're ready to take the next step.

Why must I register to develop an app?

One of the ways that Apple controls the iPhone market is by using a process that creates a unique digital signature for each app. This process requires two encrypted files containing security codes – one from Apple, one from you, the developer. Unless you "jailbreak" your iPhone, you pretty much have to use these documents any time you install an app on your device.

When a user buys your app, this process is all invisible to them. And the only way that you'll be able to see the process, and use it, is to register as an Apple iOS Developer. This process will cost you $99 but this is generally the only way to run an app you've created on your own device. We will walk you through the entire process and, when you finish, you'll be able to play your own game apps, test your apps to submit them to the App Store, and show off at parties.

The Apple Developers' Agreement

In order to use Apple's software and services, like Xcode and the App Store, you must accept the iOS Developer Program License Agreement. Like any other legal document, you should read it before you accept it. But, like any other legal document, it's pretty long and boring. We'll try to sum up a couple of key points here, but seriously, read the document.

What you can do, usually – There is a great deal of confusion about one key issue of what you can do as far as using a programming language other than Objective-C, or other programming tools besides Xcode for your app. Not very long ago, the iOS Developer Program License Agreement placed tight constraints on developers. The company was reacting to a few threats to their control of the platform – most notably Adobe Systems, who added features to their popular Flash development tool that allowed Flash developers to compile iPhone apps.

However, times have changed. Use of Adobe Flash is permitted, as are several other development tools. We'll discuss those more in Part II.

What you definitely CAN'T do – Want to get your app rejected from the App Store – and possibly lose your developer's status? Just try any of these stunts.

- Downloading and running executable code. If it seems like a virus, or any unanticipated action, you're pretty much done.
- Ignore the iPad. Sure, the iPhone is the bigger market, but iPad is the wave of the future and Apple makes them both. All apps developed for the iPhone must support compatibility mode on the iPad. This isn't a big issue; compatibility mode works a little like the iOS Simulator we're going to be using soon. It just makes an iPhone-sized window on your iPad and runs the app that way.
- Collecting data. Sure, you can do it, but the user has to be clearly informed that data will be collected and they must choose to accept that. If you don't do this, you are violating the developer's agreement and, in many jurisdictions, a lot of laws.
- Re-use content. It's common for many computer users to just do a simple Internet search when they need some content. Need a graphic for your game? A sound effect? Some music? Be careful where you get it from. There are many websites like Creative Commons (http://creativecommons.org/) where you can find content that you can use without paying any fees, legally. Search for sites like these and remember – even if you're not paying, you still have legal obligations to the creator. Look at the license and choose only content that suits your purpose.
- Crash. If your application doesn't run great, keep working on it until it does.

There's a lot more, obviously, but these are some key points to remember.

Whew! That may seem like a lot, but it's not so bad. If you don't develop bad habits as you're beginning, a lot of potential problems will never occur. But let this be a reminder, there are important reasons to use good technique when you develop a program. It's not just for the satisfaction of writing good-looking code.

How to get the iOS software development kit

Learning how to develop your game app for the iPhone is also learning about Xcode. Xcode is Apple's integrated development environment, or IDE. An IDE can do for programmers what Microsoft Office does for office workers every day – it can make it easier and faster to develop software. The same way that you can make a presentation in Office by copying bullet points out of Word and a table from Excel and putting them into PowerPoint, you can combine various tools in Xcode.

The simple version

Any Mac user can purchase a copy of Xcode using the Mac App Store for only $4.99. It's really that simple, and installs like any normal Mac applications. Keep in mind that the application isn't stored in your normal Applications folder. Instead, you'll find it in the Developer folder, at the top level of your hard drive. Click on your computer's icon in the sidebar of a Finder window to find it.

That's it. You're ready to start developing for the iPhone. You won't actually be able to run your app on an iPhone yet. We discuss this topic more in just a minute, but you will be able to run them on the iOS Simulator. This is a software application for the Mac. The iOS makes a window that looks like an iPhone on your computer. You can "install" your app and simulate finger touches with the mouse. It presents you with a pretty good idea of whether your app is working as intended or not.

The version you'll do one day

You will only be able to install your app on your iPhone once you have registered as an Apple developer. The fee to register is currently $99. If you are currently a college student there is a program called the iOS Developer University Program that can make your registration free. Check the Apple Developer website (http://developer.apple.com/) or check with your school's computer center for more information.

Before you can install your app onto your iPhone (or iPad or iPod touch) you'll need a Distribution Certificate and a Distribution Provisioning Profile from Apple. The Distribution Certificate includes personal identifier information that you've provided, in the form of a digital file that is stored in the Keychain. The Digital Provisioning Profile is a kind of digital signature that Xcode puts into projects you create. This whole process can only be completed when Apple has approved an app for distribution.

For development, however, there is a similar process that is also tightly controlled, but more flexible for the developer. You can set up an individual device and test on that specific device. For this, you only need a Development Certificate and a Development Provisioning Profile.

The Development Provisioning Profile includes your App ID, a unique device identifier called the UDID and an iPhone Development Certificate. This info must be installed on the testing device.

To show you that the process is not terribly complicated or long, we've gone ahead and registered for the program, and created a series of screen shots as we went through the process. Even if you don't need this information until later, we suggest that you at least skim through this section, so that you'll get an idea of the steps you're going to have to take.

First, you'll need an Apple ID. If you have an iTunes account, a Mobile Me account, a Ping account or an account for other Apple services, you already have an Apple ID – it consists of whatever e-mail address and password you already use to log in. However, if you plan to do any serious software development, we suggest you create a separate Apple ID just for business purposes.

How to set up your iPhone for development

Once you have set up your Apple ID and decided to take the plunge and register as an iOS developer, there are several steps you'll need to take to set up your iPhone to install your apps on the device.

Log into developer.apple.com and, on the Developer home page, there is now a resource listed as iOS Provisioning Portal. If you have not already done so, connect your device to your computer.

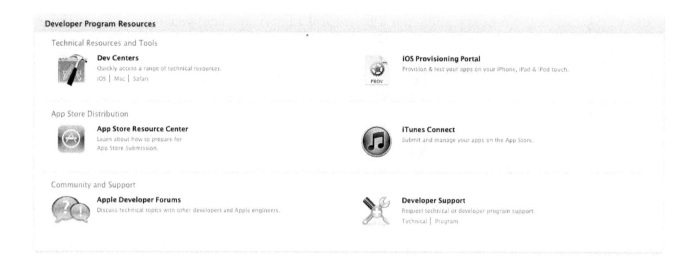

Now, let's click that link. You'll see this: "Get your application on an iOS with the Development Provisioning Assistant."

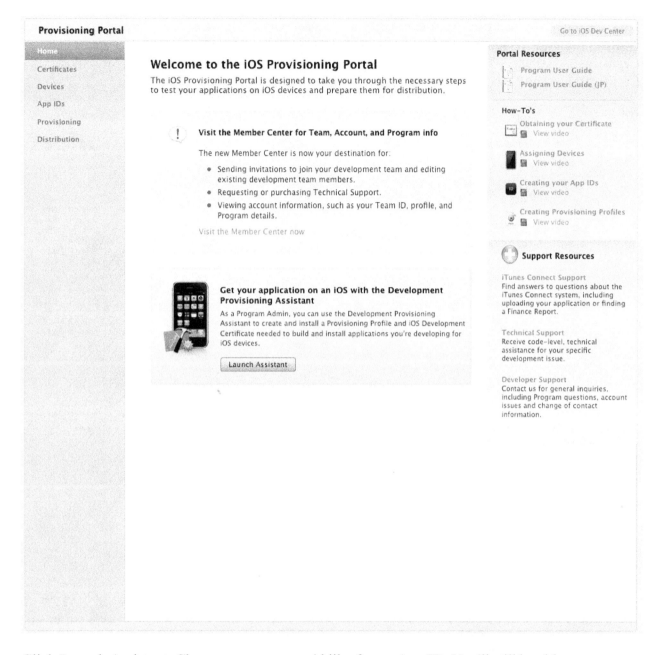

Click Launch Assistant. Choose any name you'd like for an App ID. You'll still be able to use your certificate on any projects you're working on, not just one project. Since the first tutorial is called Hello World, we chose "HelloWorld".

Next, Assign Development Device. For this example, we're calling the device TestDevice for now. To find the Unique Device ID, launch Xcode. The Organizer should recognize that your device was plugged in, and launch the Organizer window, showing your UDID. If not, you can navigate to it through Windows > Organizer. You can copy and paste that into Launch Assistant.

Now it's time to Generate a Certificate Signing Request. Go to Applications folder and open your Utilities folder, and launch Keychain Access. In Keychain Access, select Keychain Access > Certificate Assistant > Request a Certificate from a Certificate Authority. Save the file called CertificateSigningRequest.certSigningRequest to the Desktop.

When it shows the Conclusion screen, click Done.

Next, you'll have to create a Certificate Signing Request Certificate. This will generate a public and private key pair. By default, your private key will be stored on your Mac in Keychain. Your public key is your iOS Development Certificate. Click Continue.

Next, we come to Name your Provisioning Profile. Choose any name you'll easily remember and click Continue. Now, we're on to Download & Install Your Provisioning Profile.

Download your Provisioning Profile to your computer. Attach your device to your Mac. From the Finder, just drag the Provisioning Profile onto the Organizer window in Xcode. This automatically installs the .mobileprovion file in what Apple refers to as "the proper folder." Click Continue. The Organizer updates to show info about the new Provisioning Profile. Note that this Provisioning Profile expires in 90 days.

To verify that the process has completed successfully, go back to Keychain Access and select Keys. Keychain shows your public key and your private key paired together. Click the reveal arrow by your private key, and see your iPhone Developer Certificate.

Now you can install your apps on your iPhone. To test it, open a project in Xcode.

In the Project Window, select your iOS device from the Scheme drop down menu in the upper-left hand corner.

Xcode may need to collect debugging data from the device. It's a simple process, but it takes some time, like installing an update.

When Xcode fully recognizes your device, simply click the Run button in the upper left-hand corner of your Xcode Project Window, making sure your iOS device is still selected under Schemes. Xcode will build your app on your device so you can run it like any other app.

TIP: If you make changes in your app, don't just rebuild it onto your iPhone. To prevent unexpected conflicts, delete the old version directly from your iPhone first.

How the technologies work – the tools you'll use to develop apps

Alright, we've got some of the technical details out of the way. You're all set up to create an app and you'd like to start creating. We'll have a working app for you very soon, because sometimes it's best to work hands-on with a project to understand how it really works.

A lot of things are going to be new to you, including a lot of new terminology. Let's take a couple of minutes to identify these terms. That way, when we start building apps, we can all work together.

This section is designed to present you with an overview of a lot of the technology you'll be dealing with as you create your game app. One of the great things about Xcode is that it automates dealing with a lot of this technology. Apple has provided several powerful tools that you don't have to think about at all! Let's define them:

Cocoa – Cocoa is the software that helps give the Mac its unique look and feel. What windows look like, how a scrollbar works, the way you launch or close a program is all based on the software code collectively known as Cocoa. On the iPhone, you'll be using Cocoa Touch – which performs a similar function for iOS. Much of these libraries of code can be used as-is, no modification required. And, when you do have to modify it, you generally only have to change a few lines of code. By using Cocoa Touch, you app will look professional.

iOS – iOS is the operating system that powers the iPhone. It is developed by Apple. The current version of iOS as of this writing is iOS 4.3, but we have also examined iOS 5, which is currently in beta testing. Once again, iOS will supply a fair amount of the power you need to add certain features to your app. Any functions the operating system can do for you, like managing data or accessing a network, are functions you don't have to invent in your app.

Xcode – Xcode is the same tool that Apple programmers use to create Mac OS and iOS, so it's clearly a powerful application with tremendous potential. Thanks to Apple's vaunted software design skills, it's fairly easy to use a variety of powerful features. We have a section specifically focusing on Xcode and its use. The current Xcode version is 4.0.2, but we have also examined Xcode 4.2, which is currently in beta testing.

Objective-C – Objective-C is the programming language you'll be learning about in these examples. It is the programming Apple uses to create iOS and, if you're not familiar with Objective-C, it's going to be very difficult to program for the iPhone. For people who know programming, it may be enough to say that Objective-C is a strict superset of the C programming language, adding object-orientation and more modern programming features. For beginners, Objective-C has the power and speed of a raw, basic programming language, but adds modern features that make it easy to constantly develop new code and add new features.

Frameworks – If you've ever gone to a circus, a trade show or a concert while the workers were still setting up, you know exactly what a framework is. Walls, stages, roofs and floors are all made up of frames that are put into place and lashed together for stability. Then those surfaces are covered – wood planks for a stage, canvas for a tent and colorful placards for sidewalls, for instance.

In a similar fashion, frameworks are collections of software code that you can customize and use in your own code. Any customization is often as simple as putting in special names you may have used in your custom code. Key frameworks from Apple include:

- *Foundation framework* – Apple's Core Foundation framework allows you to pass data between objects. We go into objects later but trust us, this is a very good thing.
- *UIKit framework* – UIKit is the part of the code that creates most of the ways your application interacts with the user. Showing a graphic on the iPhone screen, registering when you touched the screen and what gesture you used – that's all part of the UIKit's jobs

The Apple Way – paradigms to think about

You'll also want to begin thinking about patterns now. Once again, we'll just mention a few really important topics, and then come back to talk more about them after you've had a chance to look at some code. We'll discuss the topic in detail in Part II. Still, there is a lot you can learn, even in the simple tutorial that comes first. It will even help what we do next make more sense to you.

What is a paradigm? Technology types love to throw the word around but all it means is a set of thoughts that go together. They're just ways at looking at the world. You may be a person who analyzes every detail carefully before you make even relatively minor decisions. You may be a person who's had success trusting their gut instincts and charging boldly into new adventures. We're not saying one of these ways of looking at the world is better, but these actions reflect different beliefs – different ways of looking at the world.

Most of Apple's programming concepts can be broken down into three major paradigms – *Model-View-Controller*, *Target-Action* and *Delegation*.

Delegation is probably the simplest to understand. Sometimes one piece of code is only designed to send messages. This code usually represents an interface object that your user is going to touch. All that interface object does is send a message, and your code tells it what to do. Your code is a delegate for the interface object. The beauty of this is that your code never has to interfere with the functioning of these powerful development tools. Thus you can't break them, not if you're doing things right.

How important is understanding the Delegation model? Let's put it this way; in virtually every project you create in Xcode, Xcode will automatically generate a delegate file, a file that you're expected to use. You don't have to use it, but if you're hoping to get into the App Store, you'd better have a good reason.

Target-Action is another simple, yet powerful concept. We feel it would be better called Target-Message, but nobody asked us. Since the iPhone is mostly about responding to touches that your user makes, a large portion of what any app does is to wait, patiently, for input. We've already mentioned that interface objects can send messages to a delegate. Well, most communication in programming for Apple is about sending a message somewhere. You just type the name of the code that has the information you need, and the name of the information you want. Send a message, and you'll get that data back.

Model-View-Controller is the most complex concept, so we're going to give it a major write-up in Part II, including a metaphor to make it easier to understand. But keep this much in mind – it'll be important soon. Your app does three main types of things: It takes data from the user (controller), it figures out what to do with the data the user gave it (model) and it shows some result to the user (view).

Our last stop is getting familiar with Xcode itself, and then we'll make our first app.

How to use Xcode to develop an iPhone app

What does Xcode do, exactly? People who have experience programming may find this topic silly, but when we got started, we had no idea how some of these things worked, so we understand if you're confused. The extremely short version, for those who have never done any programming, is this:

When you write programming code, you are creating a series of instructions for the computer to carry out. However, the computer can't really understand these instructions. The old saying is true – computers mostly understand 1s and 0s. After you write down your instructions, you use a *compiler* to translate them into language that's so basic even a machine can understand it.

Xcode provides you with a clear set of interface tools to help you manage all the files of instructions you create, any associated media, and connections to frameworks that you want to use. It makes it easy to send your code to the compiler and to interpret the messages the computer sends you when the code doesn't work right.

How to use Xcode to develop an iPhone app

Xcode is a tremendously powerful piece of software, designed to put a variety of features at your fingertips. It takes a little while to get used to using these features, but each one has been designed by experts to make you more productive. Mastering some basic tools will save you a lot of time.

Interface Builder – This tool is part of Xcode that allows you to design your app's user interface graphically. Many important interface elements exist as icons in a library, and you can drag those onto a representation of your app's window to add it to your project. For a long time, Interface Builder was a software application in its own right – that's how powerful these features are. The only problem was that it was sometimes difficult to make sure your updates to the Interface and the software code were synchronized. So now Interface Builder (which we'll usually just call IB) is part of Xcode and everything is neater. Apple even offers design assistance to help you make your app better looking.

iOS Simulator – This invaluable little tool does just what it says. It's a software application, stored on your hard drive, which simulates an iPhone. By using a simple Xcode command, "Run," you can launch the iOS simulator that will give you a rough idea of how you application will work, without all the hassle of actually installing the app on your iPhone. This is a great time saver, when you have lots of changes to make.

The Xcode Interface

This is a view that's about to become very familiar to you – a common working environment for programming in Xcode. Even without us drawing big, red squares around it, you probably recognized four distinct areas of the Xcode screen. We'll tell you what these areas are, so the tutorial in the next section will make more sense to you.

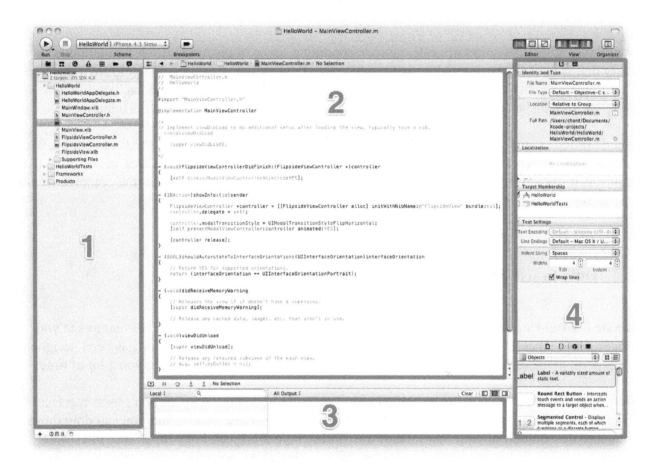

As we discuss these interface elements, follow along on your copy of Xcode, if you can. Notice that, if you hover your mouse cursor over many of the toolbar icons, a small text box will pop up, telling you the name of the icon and how it's used. This is very handy. Test it out. Select some of the different tabs and views to see how they work, and what information is presented to you.

NOTE: Don't panic if your screen doesn't look like this. Notice the three buttons grouped together towards the right hand side of Xcode's toolbar over the label View. Each of those buttons controls a corresponding portion of the Xcode window layout. You can add or remove a section by clicking the button where the corresponding part of the screen is highlighted.

1. Navigator – The Navigator works very much like the sidebar in a Finder window on your Mac. It's a simple way to get an overview of the elements that make up your software program. You can use the icons at the top to view the information in different ways. The Project navigator lets you look at an overview of the whole project (the top item in the list, with the icon that looks like a blueprint) and all of the code files, XML data, graphics, media files and XIB files associated with your project. You can look at your classes and methods with the Symbol navigator, view warnings and alerts, see debugging information and more. Clicking on any entry in a Navigator list displays the contents of that file in the Editor area.

2. Editor – The Editor is used to display data that you'll be creating, or altering, as you create your programs. Usually, that means you'll have a special text editor open that can assist you as you write your software code. However, if you're looking at an XML file, you'll probably have an easy-to-use graphical interface. And if you select a XIB file, the Editor switches to full graphic mode, showing you a representation of all of your graphical interface elements in a layout that represents what your user will see when the program runs. In this mode, the Editor is sometimes referred to as the *Canvas*.

NOTE: Notice there are three other buttons towards the right hand side of Xcode's toolbar, labeled Editor. Standard editor works in the manner described above. Assistant is a great tool for some uses – if you highlight a graphic element in your interface and then click Assistant, Xcode will open a split screen in your editor and do its best to show you a portion of your code where it expects to find instructions relating to that object. The Version editor makes it easy to compare to different versions of a file, highlighting the differences between the two in a split-screen view.

3. Debugger – The debug area is one that you will usually only use once you have written enough software code to begin to run a basic app and want to test it. Debugging is the art of catching and fixing errors in your program, and this is so important that we've got a whole section on it later. Simply put, the debugger gives you a way to see how your data changes as your program is running. If a program doesn't have major errors that make it crash, but still doesn't behave as expected, the debugger can help you figure out why.

4. Utility – The Utility area is unique in that it actually has two areas. On top is the *Inspector* pane, and on the bottom, the *Library* pane.

The Inspector pane is a place to find a huge array of information about the different objects in your code. We'll talk about objects a few times – that's how important they are – but they are the basic building blocks of your code. You'll be able to find information you'll need to use objects in your program here, including information from Apple's documentation to help you understand how the commands and keywords work.

The Library pane is simply a collection of ready-made code provided by Apple that will be helpful in creating a variety of projects. These are presented as icons that you can simply click and drag into the Editor. It's a tremendously handy tool for rapid code creation.

What will my project to look like?

When you create a new project in Xcode, several different documents will be created for you automatically. We're going to take a few minutes to look at the files that get created, what they're called and why they're created for you.

Xcode will create different files depending on what type of project you want to create. The application comes with several Apple-created templates to give you a good start in creating a new project. As a beginner, we highly recommend that you start using one of these templates. Even advanced users use them frequently.

If you are creating a View-Based Application (a very common type of app), Xcode will likely create several standard files with a name like YourProjectAppDelegate and YourProjectViewController. We'll go into a lot more detail very soon, but for now, know that the app delegate is where you put code that involves how your application interacts with the operating system – mostly the way the application starts up and shuts down. The view controller is where you will put code that processes data coming in from the user interface, and sends output to the view.

Using Xcode to write code efficiently

We've already mentioned several times that the process of writing software code is the process of trial and error, and that you will invariably make mistakes as a programmer. Well, although that's true, the good news is that Xcode has a lot of features that will help you enter your code correctly, spot errors and fix them quickly.

One great feature of Xcode is *code completion*. As we've already mentioned, there are very specific keywords that the compiler will understand, and syntax means that only certain keywords are applicable in certain circumstances. Xcode is constantly checking a list of valid keywords and, as you type, Xcode compares the letters you type to the keywords on the list and constantly pops up a list of valid commands and expressions that might apply.

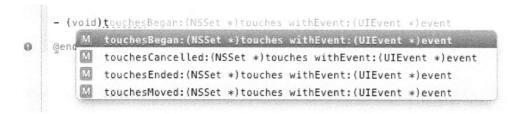

By the way, the compiler is a piece of software that translates the code you write into a language that the computer will understand quickly. You see, even though the Objective-C code you write may seem very machine-like to you, to a computer, it's still needlessly complex. Although the compiler doesn't break down the code to anything as basic as binary 1s and 0s, it does use a language that's so compressed that it would be almost impossible for a beginner to read. You don't need to directly interact with the compiler; you can start the process from Xcode, simply by clicking the Run button. The compiler will then create a version of your app and install it to either the iOS Simulator or your iPhone.

If we wanted to make your app respond when the user touches it, Objective-C for iOS already has such a method, called touchesBegan. As you can see, as soon as we type the letter "t", Xcode immediately suggests the touchesBegan method and highlights that item in its pop-up list. If you want to accept the highlighted item, just hit Enter. You can use the arrow keys to move up and down the list. As you continue to type, Xcode will narrow down the choices. By using code completion, you can type lines of code with just a few keystrokes.

You'll also notice a warning in the left margin – that red circle with an exclamation point. Remember when we said that most major lines of instructions in Objective-C end with a semicolon (;)? Well, since we are typing in new code, there's obviously not a semicolon at the end of the line yet. Until we get to the end of that line and type a semicolon, the warning will remain. It's a great way to remember to type that semicolon!

Warnings are listed on every line where there is an error so severe that your code will not compile. If the code will compile but the code involves poor design or unclear intentions, Xcode will issue an alert instead. Alerts are an exclamation point in a yellow triangle. Together, warnings and alerts are called *issues*. Clicking on the issue icon will show you more detail about the error.

NOTE: Xcode's explanations of errors can be in "computer-ese" – I.e., difficult to understand. Often, you can Google the error message, or find a more detailed explanation in the documentation.

How will this work

You'll start by creating a new project. Xcode will offer you a variety of templates to help you get started on various projects. In these examples, we will use those templates to create your projects.

Ready? Let's begin.

Tutorial 1: "Hello World!"

"Hello World" is a longstanding tradition in the world of computer programming and you're about to become a part of it. The idea is simple, really. Computers do three main things when you come right down to it. They take information in, they act based on that information, and they output information – to your screen, printer, wireless router, etc.

When teaching students about new computer technology, we often start by making it say "Hello World!" It's good for your confidence to build code right away. You'll learn something about inputting data and outputting it as well. And it's so darn friendly.

So, even though it's not a game, we're going to start by making your iPhone say "Hello world." This exercise will give you important experience using Xcode to create and run apps. You can complete this in a relatively short time, and the first time you successfully get it to run, odds are you'll be smiling.

Creating your first application

Launch Xcode. At the Welcome to Xcode screen, choose Create a new Xcode project.

Welcome to Xcode
Version 4.0.2 (4A2002a)

Create a new Xcode project
Start building a new Mac, iPhone or iPad application from one of the included templates

Connect to a repository
Use Xcode's integrated source control features to work with your existing projects

Learn about using Xcode
Explore the Xcode development environment with the Xcode 4 User Guide

Go to Apple's developer portal
Visit the Mac and iOS Dev Center websites at developer.apple.com

Xcode will present you with a screen titled Choose a template for your new project. Select Utility Application and click Next.

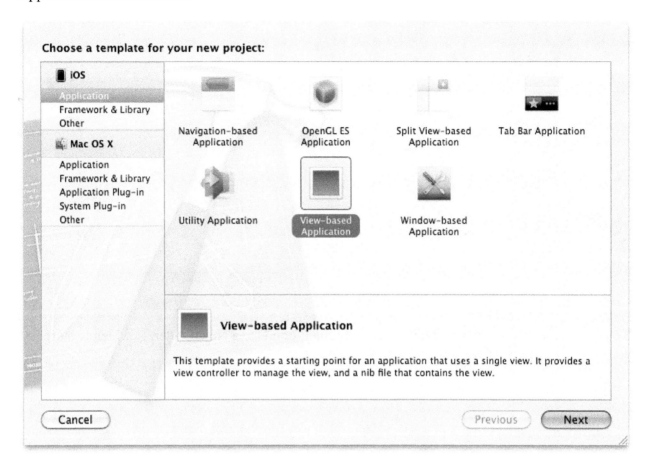

The next screen is titled Choose options for your new project. We named our project "HelloWorld." Xcode initially uses a company identifier of "com.yourcompany" and shows you what the Bundle Identifier would look like ("com.yourcompany.HelloWorld"). Don't use Core Data or Include Unit Tests. Click Next.

Choose options for your new project:

Product Name HelloWorld|

Company Identifier com.yourcompany

Bundle Identifier com.yourcompany.HelloWorld

☐ Use Core Data
☑ Include Unit Tests

Cancel   Previous   Next

You will see a standard Save dialog. Choose a folder, or create a New Folder, in which to store your project. Do not select Source Control for now. Click Create.

Select the MainView.xib and the Interface Builder canvas will come up in the Standard Editor window.

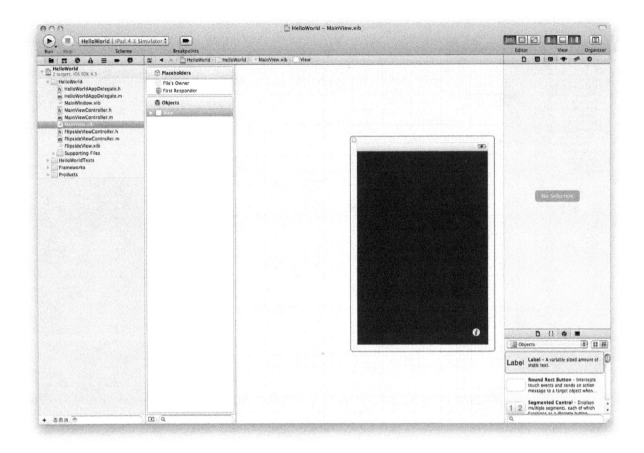

Now, we want to create our main view. Select the view in Interface Builder and see the Identity Inspector activate. That's also important because it shows the Library.

Now, look at the Library, in the lower right-hand corner of the screen. If the drop-down menu near the top of the section says anything other than "Objects," just click the Object icon (it looks like a little cube). Click on the Label item in the Objects Library and drag it on to the main view. Don't release it right away. Notice how you will occasionally see dotted blue horizontal and vertical lines temporarily appear on the screen. These are guides for your graphic design. Xcode shows you some suggested locations, based on standard interface design principle. You're not forced in any way to use them, but it's helpful to keep them in mind.

Now, let's make the label bigger, so we can read the whole message. You can do this by simply grabbing one of the handles on the label and clicking-and-dragging on it. We're going to take a somewhat more precise approach. Click the Size Inspector symbol at the top of the Inspector. Note the small graph indicated the point of origin for the size change. If you click the dot in the center of that diagram, all changes will be made outward, from the center of the object.

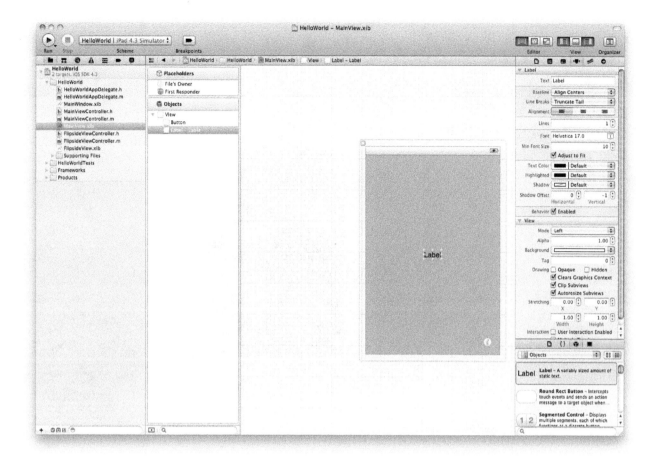

The original Label object had a size of 42 and a height of 21. We're going to double that size, to 84 by 42.

Now, it's time to create an Info page for our app. Click on FlipsideView.xib to show the flipside. Click the little reveal triangle next to View.

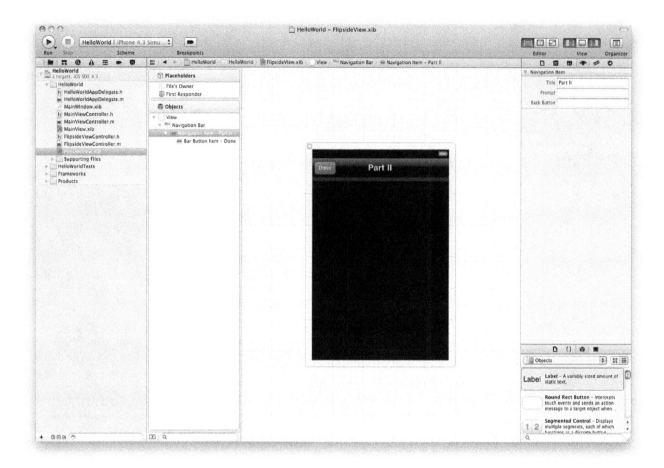

First, let's change that title to something more appropriate. This view doesn't really offer any additional information – it just expands on the first view, so we'll call it Part II. You can change the name by double clicking on the current title in Interface Builder and typing in the new title. You can also select the interface item by clicking on the object in Interface Builder (or the Dock) and entering the information in the Title field of the Attribute Inspector.

Now, drag another Label from the Object Library and drag it onto the view. Change the text color to White, so it shows against the background and change the text to "Goodbye, for now...."

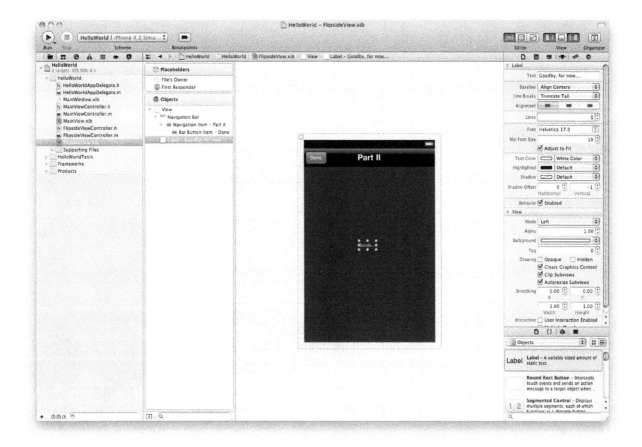

Now, resize the Label so you can see the text clearly. We used 210 by 63.

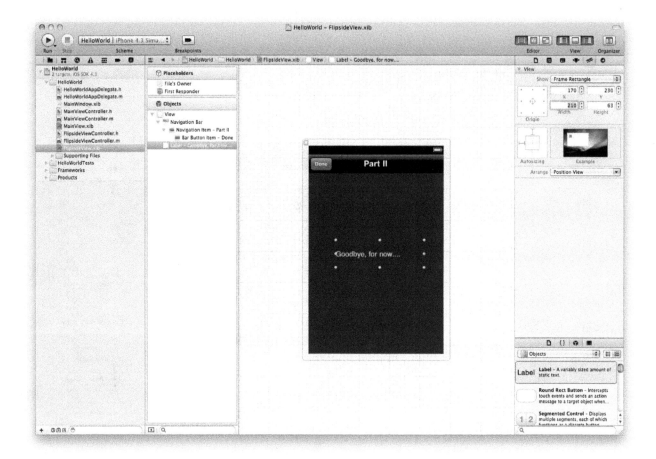

Make sure that the Scheme selected in Xcode's upper left-hand corner is set to iPhone 4.3 Simulator. Click the Run button (also in the left-hand side of Xcode's toolbar), Select Product > Run or hit Command-R.

The iOS Simulator launches and shows your app's main view. Click on the small "i" symbol in the lower right-hand corner to view the Flipside. Click Done to return to the first view.

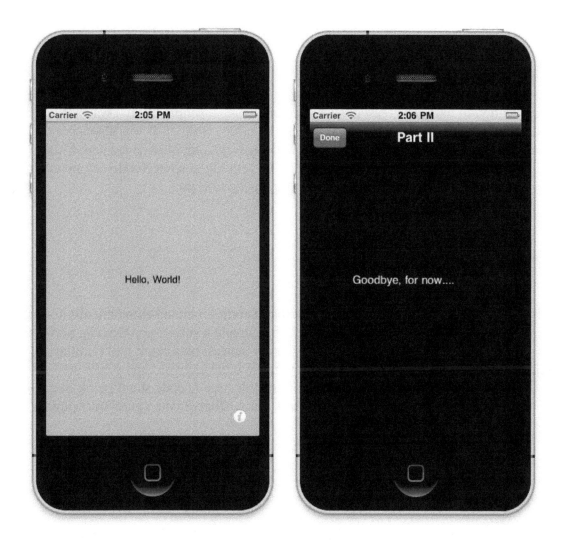

When you're finished checking out your app, return to Xcode and press the Stop button to end the simulation.

"Hello World," Xcode and Objective-C – What we just did

Alright folks, hang onto your hats. The reason we started with such a simple tutorial was not just to give you hands-on experience with Xcode, especially with Interface Builder. It was also a good way to show you some example code. You see, Xcode will generate a lot of code for you. Code created by the master Objective-C programmers at Apple. By looking at what Xcode automatically creates for you, you can learn about what kind of code you'll need to create.

Examining your Xcode project

We're going to start very simply, by looking at the code that Xcode generated automatically for you. You've already seen that this code is powerful enough to create a simple app that can perform minor functions. We're going to look at some of these files for several reasons. It will familiarize us with how Objective-C files are structured, it will show us how the keyword and syntax of Objective-C are used, and it will show us what well-written Objective-C code should look like. We're not going to go over every line and every command, but we'll give you a good overview of Objective-C in action.

An overview of your project

We've mentioned that Xcode will virtually always create an app delegate file for you. You should actually see two files with the words "app delegate" in their names – HelloWorldAppDelegate.h and HelloWorldAppDelegate.m. Xcode automatically splits the app delegate into two files. The file that ends in ".h" is called the header file and the file that ends in ".m" is the implementation file. Objective-C files are almost always split in two like this. Roughly put, the header contains code that helps define everything that this code is responsible for doing. The implementation file contains the instructions that make those actions possible.

Let's start by looking at that, to see what it does. Go to the Navigator area and select HelloWorldAppDelegate.h.

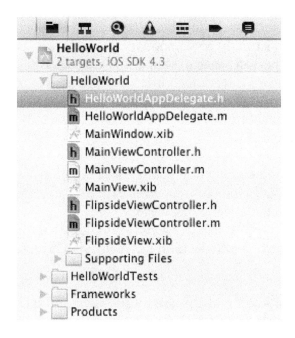

You should see code that looks very similar to this:

```
//
//  HelloWorldAppDelegate.h
//  HelloWorld
//

#import <UIKit/UIKit.h>
@class MainViewController;

@interface HelloWorldAppDelegate : NSObject <UIApplicationDelegate> {
}

@property (nonatomic, retain) IBOutlet UIWindow *window;
@property (nonatomic, retain) IBOutlet MainViewController *mainViewController;

@end
```

This may look confusing, but we'll take this line by line and, in a little while, it will make sense.

The first four lines – the ones that begin with "//" are simply comments. Any time the compiler sees a line that begins with //, it knows there are no instructions there for it, and it moves on to the next line.

Comments are a great way for you to leave comments to yourself, or to other programmers, about what the code is and what it does. We can't emphasize too strongly how important that is. When you're in the grip of inspiration, all your work may make perfect sense to you. But come back a few days later and you'll be surprised how confusing it can become. Label different sections of your code, what variables stand for and any other helpful information for future reference. Apple thoughtfully starts you off by putting the title of the document right at the top, which is very handy because you'll have to manage a lot of documents sometimes.

 # import – Using import allows you to use other code by referencing it in your project. Apple's *UIKit* is the library of code that provides all the user interface elements that users expect in an iPhone app. You will use this very frequently, so Apple automatically includes it.

@class – You actually won't be using this often so we won't go into detail. It has many similarities to import.

NOTE: All of the symbols we've discussed on these lines – //, # and @ – are special symbols that help the compiler interpret the information we're about to give it.

@interface – the interface is the section where we will put the names of any special variables or methods that should be associated with HelloWorldAppDelegate. You'll notice there is nothing in this interface – you don't need to add anything here until you start customizing your code. However, the *curly braces* ({}) following the word interface **MUST** be there.

NOTE: Curly braces must always balance – if there is a left brace ({), there must be a right (}). The same holds true for quotation marks, parentheses, brackets, etc.

@property – This is a great new function that was recently added to Objective-C. We'll talk about it more, but it essentially comes down to this. There are generally only two things you want to do with a variable – either check to see what its value is, or change that value.

For example, you want to create a Hangman-type game, where users guess the letters in a word. Every time the player guesses wrong, another part of the hanged man is drawn. The drawing will be complete after nine misses. It would be handy to create a variable to keep track of the number of guesses. Every time the player guesses wrong, the variable will be set one number higher. Every time the player guesses wrong, we want to get the value of the variable. When the value we get is 9, the game ends.

These types of programming tasks are so common, programmers speak of the instructions as *setters* (which change the value of the variable) and *getters* (which read the value of the variable). Every setter and getter is pretty similar. So, the nice people who make Objective-C decided, "why write them at all?" It's just another layer of complexity, one more area where mistakes can be made.

Now, you just declare that your variable has a property in the header file. Later, in the implementation file, you will ask the compiler to @synthesize that variable, and it creates setters and getters for you.

@end – You can probably guess this one. If you don't tell the compiler when you're done, how will it know when to stop reading the code and start running it?

There you have the code that helps set up your app delegate, by *declaring* the names that you will use in your commands. Now let's see those commands.

The implementation file

Now, as we've mentioned, there's another part of the app delegate – the implementation files, HelloWorldAppDelegate.m. It will look something like this:

```
//
//  HelloWorldAppDelegate.m
//  HelloWorld
//

#import "HelloWorldAppDelegate.h"
#import "MainViewController.h"

@implementation HelloWorldAppDelegate

@synthesize window=_window;
@synthesize mainViewController=_mainViewController;

- (BOOL)application:(UIApplication *)application
didFinishLaunchingWithOptions:(NSDictionary *)launchOptions
{
    // Override point for customization after application launch.
    // Add the main view controller's view to the window and display.
    self.window.rootViewController = self.mainViewController;
    [self.window makeKeyAndVisible];
    return YES;
}

- (void)applicationWillResignActive:(UIApplication *)application
{
    /*
```

Sent when the application is about to move from active to inactive state. This can occur for certain types of temporary interruptions (such as an incoming phone call or SMS message) or when the user quits the application and it begins the transition to the background state.

Use this method to pause ongoing tasks, disable timers, and throttle down OpenGL ES frame rates. Games should use this method to pause the game.
```
    */
}
```

```
- (void)applicationDidEnterBackground:(UIApplication *)application
{
    /*
```
Use this method to release shared resources, save user data, invalidate timers, and store enough application state information to restore your application to its current state in case it is terminated later.

If your application supports background execution, this method is called instead of applicationWillTerminate: when the user quits.
```
    */
}
```

```
- (void)applicationWillEnterForeground:(UIApplication *)application
{
    /*
```
Called as part of the transition from the background to the inactive state; here you can undo many of the changes made on entering the background.
```
    */
}
```

```
- (void)applicationDidBecomeActive:(UIApplication *)application
{
    /*
```
Restart any tasks that were paused (or not yet started) while the application was inactive. If the application was previously in the background, optionally refresh the user interface.
```
    */
}
```

```
- (void)applicationWillTerminate:(UIApplication *)application
{
    /*
```
Called when the application is about to terminate.
Save data if appropriate.
See also applicationDidEnterBackground:.
```
    */
}
```

```
- (void)dealloc
{
    [_window release];
    [_mainViewController release];
    [super dealloc];
}
```

@end

Let's briefly analyze this code. We see two import statements at the top. Logically, the implementation file needs to import the header, so that all the code works together. It also imports the main view controller, since that's where most of your app will actually "happen." The @implementation keyword just tells the compiler that this is the application part of app delegate – you'll also see the @end keyword as the last line in the file. The @synthesize keyword was discussed in the previous section.

However, we see something new and very different in this file. There are several groups of code that are each structured similarly – there is a dash, a keyword in parentheses (BOOL or void, in this example), some other series of keywords (which varies from group to group) and a lot more code in between two curly braces ({}). What are these?

These are *methods*. Methods are very important and will be discussed in detail in *Part II: More challenging projects*. For now, however, it's good to know that the compiler automatically associates all the code that appears in the curly braces with the method name that comes just before it.

In other words, all of the code in the first method – named applicationdidFinishLaunchingWithOptions – can be called and run from other parts of your code by using the applicationdidFinishLaunchingWithOptions name. As you might guess, this code is automatically called when an iPhone user taps the icon for your app, but before the game actually starts – just as it finishes launching. As the comments there already point out, that's an ideal spot to customize special features you've created for your app.

We won't go into detail about this code for now but there are two points worth emphasizing in these three simple lines. Notice that each line of code ends with our old friend, the semicolon. As we've said, get used to that. Also, notice that the middle line of code is contained in brackets ([self.window makeKeyAndVisible];). This is the unmistakable sign of a *message*.

Messages are a major technique you'll use to call other code. A message is divided into two parts. The first part of the message (self.window) tells the compiler what object the code is messaging. In this case, the keyword self indicates that the message is actually going to the process that is currently running (the ".window" portion will be discussed in Part II), the actual message is makeKeyAndVisible, which is code supplied by Apple that makes this application the main one running on that particular iPhone. As you already know, only one iPhone app is visible on screen at any time. The makeKeyAndVisible message means that right now, that app is yours.

Finally, notice the method at the end, dealloc. *This is incredibly important*. The iPhone must save space in its memory for every piece of data you are going to use in your program – that's why you have to declare names for pretty much every item you intend to use in your app (it's done in the header file, remember?). The iPhone is a powerful device but it's small. It has a limited amount of memory. To be fair to other programmers, you must release every bit of memory you reserved for your app, when your app is done. Failure to do so is bad programming and will likely get your app rejected from the App Store.

View Controller header and implementation

The Hello World app has three views – MainWindow, MainView and FlipsideView. Every app has a main view. A view is simply a graphical container, meant to hold other information. You can put a picture in a view, or other media. You can output data to a view, like numbers or sentences. The main window is predefined by Apple to tie basic behavior that is common to every app to the *GUI* – graphical user interface. You won't be working with it directly in most cases. The main view is where you'll usually work, so we'll look at MainViewController.h and MainViewController.m.

You'll notice that MainViewController.h is almost empty – there's only one new thing to see here:

- (IBAction)showInfo:(id)sender;

We've already discussed how the combination of that dash and a name indicates a method. We even saw some methods in HelloWorldAppDelegate.m. The methods used in HelloWorldAppDelegate.m, however, are pretty standard methods supplied by Apple, so we didn't actually have to declare them in the header file.

This method is something new, however. The first thing we notice is that odd keyword in the parentheses – IBAction. This tells your app that an action is supposed to take place when the user touches the ShowInfo button. And, sure enough, when you touched the Show Info button, the view changes to the flipside view. Apple also automatically supplies this code for us.

Now, let's flip over to MainViewController.m. There are several methods there, as you can see. We'll look more at the ShowInfo method so you'll understand it better:

```objc
- (IBAction)showInfo:(id)sender
{
    FlipsideViewController *controller = [[FlipsideViewController alloc]
initWithNibName:@"FlipsideView" bundle:nil];
    controller.delegate = self;

    controller.modalTransitionStyle = UIModalTransitionStyleFlipHorizontal;
    [self presentModalViewController:controller animated:YES];

    [controller release];
}
```

There are only three things we want to emphasize here for now. First, the first three lines of code basically serve to tell the view controllers how to animate the transition from the main view to the flipside. Trust us, this is exactly the kind of code you don't want to have to write. It's hard to get right, and easy to make big mistakes.

Second, you see another message – [self presentModalViewController:controller animated:YES];– which just sends a message to the controller (self) that tells it how to animate the transition.

Third, the controller that is created in the first line of the method is released in the last line.

Objective-C basics / programming basics – variables, operators, loops, conditionals, keywords

There are many different programming languages in the world and some of them vary quite widely from one another, but there are certain characteristics they will often have in common. These languages will offer you some way to create variables, operators, loops and conditionals. They will also generally use specific keywords, like commands, to perform these functions. Finally, syntax covers certain ways commands should be written. The computer has no way to understand and interpret your commands. Using proper syntax will help the compiler, and the computer, understand what you're trying to tell it to do.

Variables – Variables are simply some name that you use to represent data. Most of you remember variables from math class as the dreaded "x" you needed to solve. For instance, $5x = 10$ – what, times five, equals 10? The answer, of course, is that x equals 2.

Variables are important because they allow you to use your code more than once. Here's another example. In the U.S., 15% is a common amount for tipping a server in restaurants. It's very easy to figure out what the tip should be on your favorite meal (which just happens to cost $10) by using the following formula – $10 * 15% = $1.50 (we use * for multiplication instead of x, so it won't be confused with the variable x, if used). You could easily write a computer program to figure it out – although we're not certain why you'd bother.

But what if the cost of your dinner changes? What if you go out with friends and everyone orders different meals? Your program would become useless. But not with the magic of variables. Instead of using the fixed price of $10, you could create a variable called costOfDinner. Using a formula like costOfDinner * 15%, all you'd have to do is enter the cost of the dinner, and you'd get an output of the correct tip amount.

You could go even further by creating another variable called percentTip. If the custom of $15% tipping ever changes (to 10%, say, or 20%) you just enter the cost of your dinner and the percentage you want to tip and you have the correct answer for a variety of situations. Much more useful.

Operators – We use mathematical operators every day – multiplying, dividing, adding and subtracting. These are commonly used in programming as well – "*, /, + and -". They work much the way you're used to.

You'll find some other key operators that are also handy. You'll have to learn them because they're not as obvious. For instance && is used to create the logical comparison AND. Similarly || means logical OR. Taking a variable and doubling an arithmetic operator like + or - makes a convenient way to increment or decrement a counter variable. By writing something like counter++, the variable counter (if it is a number) will be increased by one.

TIP: One common operator, of course, is the equal sign. Here is one place where you'll have to be very careful. One equal sign (=) is used to assign a variable (a = 5, assigns the value five to the variable a). To check if two things are equal, we will use a double equal sign (==) Using this example to make sure the value of a is five, we would check if a == 5.

TIP: When you write a formula, you'll want to remember to use parentheses to group the expressions together. It is better to write (x * y) + (a * b) instead of x * y + a * b. The computer will always do the math in parentheses first.

Loops – Loops are a key element of game programming. Later in this guide, we'll be doing a version of the classic arcade game Pong. The ball needs to constantly stay in motion. The way we will do this is to create a loop.

A loop is very much what it sounds like: A series of actions that are performed over and over again. In fact, the entire iOS works a little like a loop. It constantly checks to see if the user has touched the screen. Most loops come in two flavors – for loops and while loops. A for loop generally works on a specific count. For an app that flipped through a deck of cards, you might want to run a loop that showed a card for every number from one to 52. For an app that worked like an emergency light, you might want the screen to glow while the user kept pressing the button.

Conditionals – So much of programming comes down to two choices. Think about dialog boxes you get every day, giving you the choice to Save or Cancel, to Abort or Retry, to Accept or Reject.

The most common way to create a conditional is by using the word if. It works much like you might expect. When you use an if statement, you will then supply a condition. If that condition is met, the code is executed. If it is not, the next block of code is run. For instance, if you were making a baseball game, three strikes would indicate an out, and three outs would signify the end of an inning.

If you created a variable like counter (see above), and incremented it for every out, then you would want to change sides if counter == 3.

Keywords – Keywords are words that have specific meaning in the world of software programming. Many are commands but others also have specific meaning. These words are reserved – they can't be used as variable names or for any other purpose except the ones for which they were intended.

We've already talked about several of them – for, while and if. Others include commands to output data, like print. You'll also learn some highly specialized words. When you create a user interface element in Interface Builder (IB) that you need to connect to your code, you will declare an IBOutlet. When you need to declare a variable to store an integer, you'll declare an NSInteger.

We'll be covering this in great detail during this guide, but you might as well start getting used to it now.

Syntax (and punctuation) – In English, syntax is the skill of constructing sentences properly. It means little things that help the user understand. When you say, "I went to the store," you put the subject ("I") first, the verb second and the object (the store) last. Someone listening to you can quickly figure out what you're talking about.

Computers are much dumber than people, so they need all the help they can get. All the code you write will be influenced by syntax, and there are several aspects to learn. However, some things are so vitally important that your program won't even run until these are correct. Let's talk about those keys for now.

The first thing to understand is the importance of the semicolon (;). Many people hardly even use it while writing English, which may be why it's used so much in programming. In Objective-C, most lines of code that send a command to the computer end in a semicolon. Much like a period (.) in an English language sentence, the semicolon tells the computer that the command has been fully expressed. Without that ending mark, the computer will not understand the command is complete. Many, many errors in programming can be traced back to that simple mistake.

Another key issue to be aware of is that of punctuation that contains specific data – like quotation marks, parentheses, brackets ([ ]) and "curly braces" ({ }). These must be "balanced"; there must be a left bracket ([ ) for every right bracket ( ]). If these punctuation marks do not balance, your program will fail.

There are many syntax-related issues to discuss but these are the fundamentals. Even experienced programmers make these simple errors and they are certain to happen to you too. Learning to look for these will make it easier to prevent errors before they happen, and fix them if they do occur.

How to get into the App Store

One of the things that many fledgling developers don't realize is how easy it is to submit your app for review to be added to the App Store. Any registered developer is eligible, be they from a big company or an individual developer. That doesn't mean you'll get in, however.

Still, your odds are good if you only remember a few simple things. Your app is likely to make it in, so long as you don't specifically do something wrong. After all, Apple takes 30% of the price paid for every app sold in the App Store. Your success is their success.

However, Apple wants high-end professionals developing for the iPhone. Those developers will be embarrassed if their work is sold alongside shoddy, substandard apps. That's why some apps get rejected. If your work is polished and tested, you can get into the App Store.

Why some apps get rejected

At Apple's developer website (http://developer.apple.com/), you can read the App Store Review Guidelines. Fortunately for those of us who are less legally inclined, they also do a short summary of the key points:

- Apple looks for apps that are original
- If your app is aimed at kids, expect special scrutiny
- Your app should be attractively designed, and the code should run smoothly, without crashing or interfering with other apps, or the operation of the iPhone
- If your app is too edgy – violent, sexual, scatological, rude or offensive – it may get rejected. Although you can appeal to a Review Board if this is the case
- If your app steals content or code, it will be rejected
- If Apple believes your app is trying any shady behavior, it will be refused – stealing data, making unauthorized transactions, faking reviews, manipulating user ratings will all get you canned from the App Store.

How to submit your app for approval

When you believe your app is finally ready, you'll need to submit your app to Apple for review. That's a little beyond the beginner scope so we're not going to walk through the process here. However, you'll be happy to know that the process is relatively streamlined these days, through an Apple tool called iTunes Connect.

The tool is web-based, creating an easy interface to connect directly to Apple. Use iTunes connect to set up accounts for yourself and other developers who may be working with you. You can make sure you receive e-mail alerts for any information relating to your account.

You can submit your app to Apple, check on its review status, get sales numbers, banking info and tax information, all through iTunes Connect. Registered iOS Developers can register for iTunes Connect through the Developers' website.

Part II: More challenging projects

Modern programming: It's all about the objects

There are plenty of myths about programming – that it's incredibly hard or, secretly, childishly simple, for instance. But we know this much – modern programming is about paradigms and objects.

A paradigm is simply a way of thinking. More specifically, it's about a group of thoughts that go well together. Consider how much of the modern computer, its interfaces and names refer to things in a common office. Users create documents, sometimes called files. They store those files in folders. Sometimes these folders are kept on our desktop. Heck, Microsoft even calls one of its biggest-selling products Office.

Earlier, we explained what a framework was by describing people putting up a rigging for a concert stage or a circus tent. Analogies like these are powerful tools to help us understand what can be, at heart, an esoteric process.

If you are unfamiliar with object-oriented programming, think about a conveyor belt instead. In a factory, five workers make a table. One worker places the tabletop on the belt, with the holes for the legs facing upwards. The other four workers each put in one leg apiece, always using the same spot on the tabletop. We'll call the holes for the table legs positions 1, 2, 3 and 4. At the end of the conveyor belt, one last worker places the table on a palate, where it's taken to a showroom floor.

Now, none of these workers need to know each other. They don't have to be friends, or follow the same sports team, or even speak the same language. These workers only have to do a specific job. If the worker who puts the tables on the conveyor belt needs a day off, another worker can substitute, as long as they put tables on the conveyor belt and put them right side up.

Now, think about software. There are many tasks that all sorts of programs have to do. They all have to start up when you double-click their icon. Many of them need to open files from your hard drive and save them. Many need to connect to the Internet. It would be foolish for every programmer to write this code over and over again, so you can create software that works like an object. It does one type of function to one type of data. That's a simplification, but you get the idea.

If you need to get data from a URL for your game – like the user has to log in to an online game, Apple has an object that will help you. You pass that object the information it needs – the URL – and it hands you back the data you requested. That's all you need to know about that object. That's all you'll ever need to know about that object.

Classes, objects, properties and methods

Now let's connect that analogy to some programming language. Much of the task of programming is broken down into creating your code in certain ways. It's helpful to think this way, while you're thinking about your code.

Classes – Classes are groups of code that only exist to create objects. In our example, you can think of the whole description of the assembly line as a class, called Factory, which produces "table" objects. Rarely will you interact with classes to directly affect the way they work. The person who creates the class creates an interface, which we've discussed before. You supply what the class needs and the class generates an object. This is important for *reusability*. You could send the Factory wood parts, plastic parts or metal parts and you'd still end up with a table – just a different table. Each table would work just the same, however.

Objects – We've already talked about objects a bit. Objects are groups of data and instructions that are frequently used to represent something in the real world – even if it's only an abstract concept.

For instance, if you created an online, multiplayer game, you would need to have a record of every registered player. You'd need to store their user name, password, character name, whether that user is currently logged in, and the stats for the player character.

Once you decided what data you wanted to use, you would create a class called something like RegisteredUser. When a new user registered, you would send all that data to your RegisteredUser class and it would produce a unique object representing that user. There would be one unique object for every user. Each user object could be used in the exact same way.

Properties – There can be some confusion here, because of the @property keyword we discussed earlier. This concept is not related to that keyword. There are a few different phrases that may be used for this concept but "properties" is the most common. Properties are simply the various data that makes each object unique. In other words, since we have different names, user names and passwords, our user objects could be easily distinguished from each other with just a little examination. Well, every type of data that you will collect for every object that has a distinct value (name, age, address, Social Security number, etc.) is a property. In my user object, the name property has a value of "John Doe." In yours, the value of the name property is "Jane Smith."

Methods – Methods are the key concept that brings extra power to object-oriented programming. After reading the description for properties above, you might think an object isn't much different than a record in a spreadsheet or a database. Methods are a series of instructions that are associated with every object created by a specific class, usually defined in that class. This keeps commands that you might want to run on certain types of data together with the data that you would like to use with those commands.

To stay with the same example, say your online, multiplayer game charges customers a monthly subscription fee. You would want to allow users to quit the game and no longer get billed monthly. Similarly, if a user stops paying their subscription you would want to cancel their access, even if they haven't quit.

With methods, all you would have to do is define a method, let's call it cancelUser, that will change the user name and password in such a way that the user can no longer log in. When a user quits, or doesn't pay, your program could run that method on that unique user. The user would be locked out, but all other users would be unaffected.

Combined, these are very powerful concepts. They give you a way to create programs more efficiently and quickly. Even better, the more apps you create, the more code you'll invent that can be used again in future projects because of reusability – making you even faster and more efficient as time goes by.

The Model-View-Controller Paradigm

Finally, there's one other paradigm you'll want to be aware of if you want to write software for the iPhone. That is the model-view-controller paradigm, or MVC. MVC is a series of thoughts about how you should structure your thoughts and your code. It provides a way to keep several complex operations simpler, by separating them.

Remember when we said that computers basically do three things – take in information, perform some function on the data it has been given, and output that information? Then you're already partway to understanding MVC.

Our analogy this time is watching your TV. Imagine yourself in your most comfortable couch or easy chair, with a beverage and a snack, ready to watch some favorite shows. We're going to take these ideas a little out of order, so bear with us for a moment.

We do that because the controller in this system is the easiest part to understand – it's your remote control. The buttons can change the volume, the channel or even help you search for upcoming shows, if you have an information channel. It can pick broadcast TV or – if you have them – cable, DVR, DVD player or other options.

The TV is your view. Any data that comes in is displayed on the view. It can be a movie, or a show, or the program guide, or a help screen. The view shows whatever it is given.

The idea of the model is more complex. The model is the whole industry that lies beyond your wall and your house, at the other end of your cable. The cable company (or the broadcasters) sends movies, sitcoms, news, documentaries and more. These shows require writers, actors, directors, animators, designers, technicians and many more specialists to create the content. Lawyers, agents, accountants and network executives buy, sell and schedule this content.

Now, to see what this can mean to your programming, look at it this way. Your local broadcast stations don't care who is watching or what they're watching. They have information to broadcast so they do. However, at home, watching TV, you can change the model entirely. You can watch a show on cable, on DVR or on DVD. The view and the controller still work exactly the same way. The TV turns on and off the same way it always did and the volume can still go up and down. You can still use your buttons on the controller to do those things exactly the way they did when you were watching broadcast TV.

Similarly, if you get a new TV, you just unhook the old one and hook up the new one. It should work much like the old one did. That's the important part of MVC – if you change one part of your software, the rest of the software should still work the same. If you isolate the model, view and controller, it becomes easier to fix mistakes, catch them before they become a problem, or not make them at all.

Programming with Objective-C

We don't assume that you have any previous experience programming computers. Of course, you do now – you've just created a program using Objective-C. This powerful, modern programming language is a mainstay at Apple.

Obviously, you won't get too far until you learn how to add custom code of your own, and that's what we're going to discuss in the next section. But we're going to start talking about the concepts now. As you've already seen, understanding the concepts is as important to learning this technology as memorizing a bunch of details.

Part of the reason we say Objective-C is a modern programming language is that it supports object-oriented programming (or, *OOP*). We talked about objects just moments ago, and we're going to get into more detail in the next section, but we want to make sure you're familiar with these concepts first. We'll be using the files you created in the first tutorial, so it'll be easy to follow along.

There are several sections in this book about Objective-C, and each one will add new topics that apply to the tutorials we'll be working on.

You're going to have to study Objective-C to truly master it. The one tough thing about learning Objective-C is that many tutorials you find online assume that you already know the C programming language. And, indeed, understanding C is part of understanding Objective-C. Still, there are reference materials designed just for the beginning Mac programmer. We particularly recommend Cocoa Dev Center (http://cocoadevcentral.com/) for its beginner's tutorials on C and Objective-C specifically for Apple developers.

Part of the Grand Design – develop your game app right, the first time

Alright. We've mentioned design patterns and we've used them. We've seen some of these patterns demonstrated in the app you created. The one last, key element to understand is how we will use these patterns when you create your own code.

Design Patterns

Model-View-Controller

We've already discussed how key it is to have an understanding of the MVC paradigm to successfully create software for your iPhone. You've also seen how using Apple's interface objects helps you strictly enforce this paradigm in your code.

All the elements of the interface make up your view. These items will display information to the user when your code tells them what data to display. These interface objects have no computing ability and, in this paradigm, they never should. Xcode will frequently create both a view and a view controller for your project, when you make a new project.

The logic of your program is the model, and you will use the view controller to send data to your view.

Delegation

Much like Xcode can automatically create a view and a view controller for you, it performs another key service by creating an app delegate. You'll recognize it easily because it will always have the name of your projects and the words "AppDelegate" for a name.

In this file, you will find methods Apple has provided to help you communicate with the your app's user interface. The interface will send messages when the user interacts with it. You write code that does something when that message is received.

That's all. Using this system, you can make many decisions about how to design and implement a user interface that looks good and runs worry-free, in minutes instead of hours or days.

Target-Action

Just a moment ago we talked about messages. Well, messages are a big part of the Target-Action paradigm. The main thing to understand here is that the basic form of a message is simple. In between two square brackets, you place the name of the target and then a blank space and the name of the action you want it to take, like so – [target action]. We'll go into more detail soon.

How design patterns make life easier

You may ask yourself, why all this focus on paradigms and design patterns? After all, any code that works is good code, right?

The answer is no. We've already mentioned that the process of programming is one of trial and error. So, over the years, these paradigms have popped up for one major reason – the more you group together related code, the easier it is to determine where an error is and how to fix it. This makes trial and error shorter and less frustrating

For instance, say your program is designed to perform a series of complex calculations and then write some data to the iPhone screen. You write some code with no obvious errors (i.e., it compiles and runs) but no data appears on the screen. Well, all the code that creates the screen is from Apple and you never touched that code, so the error isn't there.

So the error is either in the code that performs the calculations (it never returns a result) or the code that sends the message to the screen. This is easy to test. Write some code that doesn't even do any calculations – it just contains a sentence, like "Hello World", and send that to the code that is supposed to update the screen. If the message appears, your calculations are the problem. If the message doesn't appear, the problem is the code that sends results to the screen.

Now, if you had split up the jobs – if every calculation sent its individual results to the screen – it would be more difficult to find the error. Even worse, what if some of the data appeared but other parts of the data didn't? You have to check every single calculation to see what the results were, whether each was working properly and whether any combination of results was interfering or conflicting with the others. That's a lot more difficult.

Using design patterns in your game app

Understanding the design patterns that you can use in your app is the key to understanding how to make your job as a programmer simpler. We're going to take a look at some of the common tasks you'll do as you create game apps, and how Xcode helps automate those tasks for you.

Creating a graphical user interface

To create the graphical user interface, or GUI, for your application, you'll need to use the Interface Builder (IB). You can access IB by simply clicking on any file in your project with a XIB extension.

Handling touch events

One of the reasons for the success of the iPhone (and other iOS devices) is their ability to handle touch events. Users quickly learned how to interact with their iPhones by tapping, dragging and swiping.

Changing the display

Because the screen of an iPhone is so small, you can't cram too much information on there. Also, it may not be efficient to try to redraw the screen to represent a wide variety of data. It's simpler programming, and better design, to simply change to a new screen. It's important to be able to change screens quickly so your user doesn't become frustrated.

Interacting with the user

Up until now, we've talked about how you can interact with the user through Apple's interface objects – how those objects can send messages so your app knows what to do. Now, we're going to talk about the code that you're going to have to create.

There are many ways that you, as the programmer, will use to interact with your user. Since Apple has created most of the GUI programming for you, you can afford to focus most of your attention on programming what's sometimes referred to as the "logic."

Think of your program's logic as the code that makes your program special. Many of the common behaviors have already been created for you. What do you want your app to do that's unique – that you *have to* write code for, because not everybody has done this before?

By seeing and understanding some of the types of programming that you will use to solve simple problems, you'll have a better idea how to create your program's logic.

Reading and storing data

For beginners, we're not going to talk about creating data files to save to the user's iPhone or read that user's personal information. Those aren't topics for beginners to tackle. There are many missteps a new programmer can make here and almost any of them will get you rejected from the App Store.

However, there's other information you can store that can be useful in creating a great game experience. You can use variables to store information like a player's score. You can also use variables to store information from one game session to another, so the user can pick up the game exactly where they left off.

Performing simple calculations

Simple calculations are the heart of programming. Even the earliest computers were very good at basic mathematics like adding, subtracting, dividing and multiplying. If you are creating a counter so the player wins once they reach a certain score, you're simply adding one every time. When the player has to beat a countdown timer, you're simply reducing the number by one every time.

Hands-on with Objective-C

We're not going to spend a lot of time delving into history here, but it's always nice to put things in a little perspective. The language builds on the strengths of the C programming language. C has been powering some of the most sophisticated software in the high-tech industry. As you may have already guessed, Objective-C adds the object-oriented programming capabilities to C that hadn't yet been invented when C was created.

In our next tutorial, we're going to have to write custom code, so we can make a much more sophisticated app – our first working game. Before we get our hands dirty with a little Objective-C code, it's time to get a much better understanding of how all of this works.

In any kind of programming, attention to detail is vital. Even the simplest typographical error can mess things up. Transposing letters, misspellings, using a capital letter when you meant to use a lowercase letter (Objective-C is *case-sensitive*) and other errors. Punctuation is vital. Remember to look for these things as you type your code.

There is only one way to master Objective-C and that's too study it. We can provide a good overview and also tell you specifically about the code you'll use in these tutorials. You'll have to study it extensively, however, and learn it well if you want to program. Although there are some free resources online, you'll probably eventually end up investing in a beginner's book just on that topic, or even a class. Apple provides a great deal of documentation at its developer website and in Xcode itself, but a lot of Apple documentation assumes you already know how to program in C.

How Objective-C header files are constructed

As you've already seen, every major code file in your project is actually split into two files. We're going to take a minute to consider both the header and the implementation file.

There is certain information that should always be included in your header file. If you have created custom methods, you will declare them in your header file (usually near the bottom, but before "@end"). Most of the major objects you'll work with are in the program – especially *user interface* (UI) elements. If you have variables, you'll usually need to declare them as well. Finally, you'll want to declare any *IBOutlets*. Just as IBAction allows the interface to send a message to your code, IBOutlet allows your code to send data to an interface object.

Remember when we looked at the code that Xcode produced for the Hello World tutorial? The interface in the header file that we examined was empty. That's because there were no special, custom variables associated with that program. In the games we're going to create, that won't be the case. In games, you'll have custom graphics, moving objects, counters, loops and other variables. That's a lot for a computer to keep track of.

We'll help the compiler out by declaring a *namespace* for the custom objects that we're going to introduce. A namespace is a specific part of the computer's memory that keeps track of some specific variable on your instructions. When you declare a variable, you create a namespace. Later, you assign data to that namespace, like a number, a word or a picture.

We've already discussed using properties and declaring methods – we'll be using all of these in the tutorial that comes next.

How Objective-C implementation files are constructed

The first two lines of your implementation file will usually be very similar in nature. In the first, you'll import the corresponding header file, so all the information is together in the compiler. The second is simply the keyword @implementation followed by the name of your class (the part of the filename that precedes the ".h" or ".m").

As we've already seen with words that begin with the "@" symbol, this @implementation keyword is a signal to the compiler. It just tells the compiler to look here for information on the variables and methods declared in the header. The compiler will continue to look through this code for data and instructions until it find the keyword @end, which you should put at the end of each implementation file (Xcode will normally do this for you).

Methods – the power to make the computer act

Method Syntax

Methods are groups of instructions that are specifically defined within the class. Because they're defined within the class, the methods you create there will be available to any object created by the class. Any time you *call* a method – i.e., cause that code to run – the computer will act, based on those predetermined instructions.

There is a specific syntax used to create a method – we saw it in Hello World. In the header, you will usually have to declare any custom methods you create. The form is pretty standard. From Hello World, you may recall a method that Xcode created to make the Info button on the main screen:

- (IBAction)showInfo:(id)sender;

The minus sign shows that this is a specific kind of method called an instance method. There is another type of method called a class method (which is signified by a + instead of a -) but we won't be covering those. The next information is the *data type* that the method returns.

Data types are such an important concept that we're going to stop so we can go into more detail right now. Computers handle a lot of different data – most commonly expressed as some kind of number, some combination of letters, a true or false condition or "*raw data*" (like a picture, movie, audio file, web page, etc.).

However, not all types of data work the same way. You can add or divide numbers, you can search a document to see if it contains a specific word or you can compare two images by file size and dimension. But those comparisons become meaningless with the different data types – you can't add two movies and it would be pointless to compare the file size of two equations.

That's why Objective-C has data types. Some of the most prominent ones are – *char*, *byte*, *int*, *float*, *double*, *short*, *long*, *long long* and *BOOL*.

Char – Stands for character. This represents the alphabet, plus special characters like exclamation points and question marks.

Byte – Byte is eight bits (1 or 0). It's the smallest increment of data you can handle in Objective-C.

int, *float*, *double*, *short*, *long* and *long long* – These are all numbers, in order of increasing complexity. Int are the regular "counting numbers" or positive integers (1, 2, 3, ...). Floats are numbers with one decimal point. A double has two – very good for financial transactions. Short, long and long long indicate progressively larger amounts of digits stored, behind the decimal point.

BOOL – BOOL, sometimes called Boolean, is a truth test. It will either return YES or NO as a value. This is very good for testing to see if a variable is included in a list of values. The great thing about BOOL is that it is a very small data type, so you can store plenty of them.

The importance of typing can't be overemphasized. Frequently, when you are trying to pass data to another part of your code and you get an error message – typing is the culprit.

...Back to our discussion of methods

So data type is a key way to determine how Objective-C treats your data. Certain functions are only available for specific data types – you can only multiply numbers, for example. To get back to the code we were just looking at:

- (IBAction)showInfo:(id)sender;

We now see this is an instance variable and its type is IBAction . The colon shows that we are going to send some information. In this case, we send the identity of the sender. Use IBAction (same as void) to alert Interface Builder of an action:

More on messaging

We've already seen how messages are used to call other code in Objective-C. You'll be doing a lot of that, so we'll look at that topic in more detail. The basic form is pretty simple. For instance, "[object method]" where object is the name of an object in your program and data is the name of a method to be run. If it's a method that requires data to store, modify or analyze, we pass the data in as an argument, like so – "[object method: argument]".

Sending messages nested inside messages is common. For instance, "NSString *operation = [[sender titleLabel] text];" sends a message to the button, asking for its title label. Then it sends a message to the title label, asking what that label says (its text).

Reading left to right, this says that a string called operation sends a message to the title label, asking it for its text. Each argument follows the method. Objective-C does that, so that good Objective-C code will read like English, in identifying the object to be passed, to a human reader.

Instance Variables

When you create your variables, you can define how easy or hard it is to access that variable from outside the class. By default, their scope is @protected. This is sufficient to work on these tutorials. As you become more sophisticated, you should generally use @private.

If you allow other programmers to access variables inside your program, you leave yourself vulnerable if they exploit some flaw in your programming. If you use @property and "*dot notation*" to access instance variables in a safe, secure, inheritable way, *dot notation* allows you, or some other programmer, to find out the value of an object's property by using a simple form like - objectName.propertyName.

Here's some example code, showing how to create methods to set/get an instance variable's value (getter takes no arguments).

```
@interface MyObject : NSObject
{
@private
    int counter;
}
- (int) counter;
- (void) setCounter:(int)anInt;

@end
```

Naming conventions can make it easier to understand the dense and sometimes cryptic world of software code. For instance, classes in Objective-C should normally be capitalized – methods and objects normally start with a lowercase letter.

With setters and getters, the tradition is that the getter is just the name of the property. The property in this example is counter. The setter is always setCounter. It has to have a capital letter. That is why we always have instance variables with a lowercase letter:

```
someObject.counter = someValue // set the instance variable
int counterValue = someObject.counter; // get the instance variable's current value
```

Properties

You can get the compiler to generate set/get method declarations with @property:

```
@property int counter;
```

– replaces:

```
- (int) counter;
- (void) set counter:(int)anInt;
```

Making the final code:

```
@interface MyObject : NSObject
{
@private
    int counter;
}
@property int counter;

@end
```

Foundation Framework

We've talked about the basic data types that are part of Objective-C. There are many other data types you can use and Apple supplies many of them. Much of this technology became part of Apple when Apple bought another software development company called NextStep. That's why all these names start with the letters "NS."

Part of what the Foundation framework offers are tools that work very much like the more basic data types, but they offer a lot more power and variety. These objects include data types such as – NSObject, NSString, NSMutableString, NSNumber, NSValue, NSData, NSDate and much more.

NSObject – Base class for pretty much everything

NSString – Probably the next most important object. NSString is immutable – you can't re-write the data. You'll want to make methods that return a new string, based on your code-based transformation. Example:

display.text = [display.text stringByAppendingString:digit];

NSMutableString – If needed. Generally only used if a string is going to be constantly and rapidly updating. Mostly use NSString

NSNumber – Object wrapper around primitives like int, float, double, BOOL, etc.

NSValue – Generic object wrapper for other non-object data types. Often, these data types come from C, like points and structs.

NSData – This data type is a great grab bag for unstructured data – web pages, images. iOS features lots of tools to convert, pass and change data.

NSDate – You can ask current date and time, store date, past or future – good for reminders or determining the "last edited" date. See also NSCalendar, NSDateFormatter, NSDateCoomponents

Tutorial 2: Tic Tac Toe

Tic Tac Toe is a great game for beginning programmers. Almost everybody is familiar with the rules, and the rules and scoring are very simple.

We're going to go through this Tic Tac Toe tutorial step-by-step, with pictures. When you finish this tutorial, you should be able to build and run this game in the iPhone simulator. If you have an iPhone or another iOS device, you'll be able to actually run this on your iPhone. It wouldn't pass muster to get into the App Store, however. But before we're done, you'll be able to know what it takes to get an app approved.

At the end of this tutorial, you'll see the actual TicTacToeViewController files we used to build and run the examples that you see here. They will be especially useful if you are unsure where to put code from this chapter.

We urge you to enter the code by hand. It will be quick, using Xcode's code completion feature, and it's important to get a feel for how code completion works. It's also good to see the different colors Xcode uses to color code your syntax, and see where Xcode pops up alerts and warnings.

Tic Tac Toe – thinking about design

We've spent a lot of time talking about objects and classes and methods. We've talked about how to think in design patterns and how this relates to the interface elements that Apple provides. Now it's time to put all of that together. Before we start slapping code into our project, let's think about what our final result should be, what actions the app needs to perform and how that relates to design patterns.

So, let's take a minute to think about this. What do we want? We want a board with nine spaces. Those spaces should be able to be an X, O or blank. So all we need it to display is a view for the board and views for each cell. We need to have logic that will respond to a touch event to change the display in that cell.

Your programming project will always go more quickly and smoothly if you think about your goals and how they fit into design patterns first.

Create a new project, choose the View-Based Application template. Name the project TicTacToe.

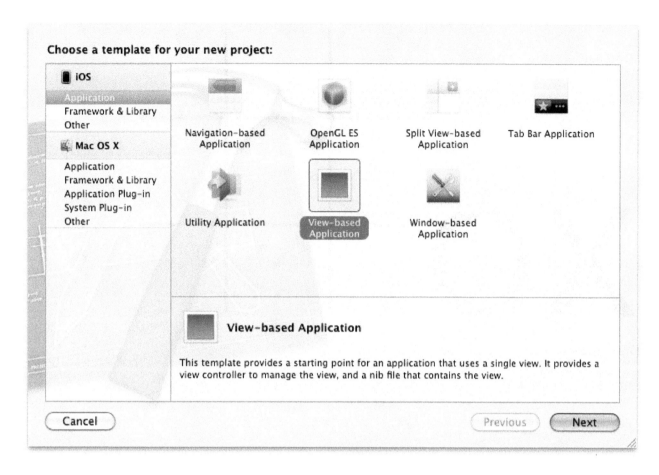

Now we're going to add the graphics. You don't have to be some type of artist to create them. For our X and O, we simply typed a capital X in TextEdit and the used formatting to make it as large as we could. We took a screenshot of the X (Command-Shift-4) and then opened the resulting PNG file in Preview. You can use the Tools > Adjust size... feature to size them exactly. We used the geometric drawing tools in LibreOffice to draw the board (OpenOffice and MS Office would do just as well). Our final results looked like this:

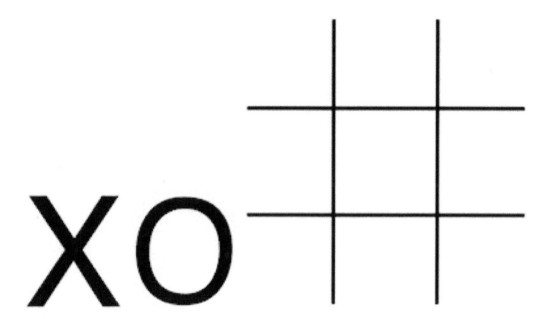

Drag them over, accept the dialog.

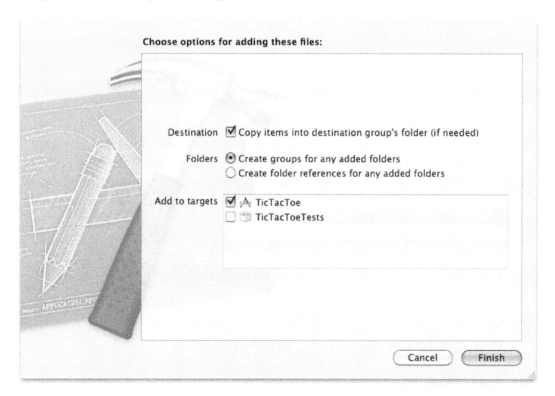

Now, select TicTacToeViewController.xib.

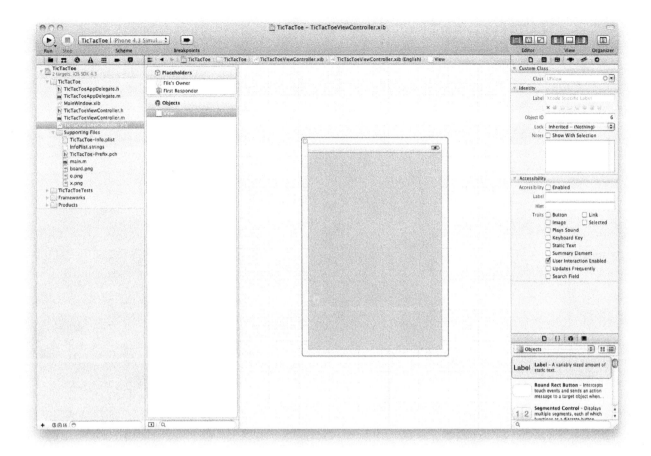

Drag an Image View on there and resize it to 300 by 300 pixels. Name it "board" in Identity Inspector.

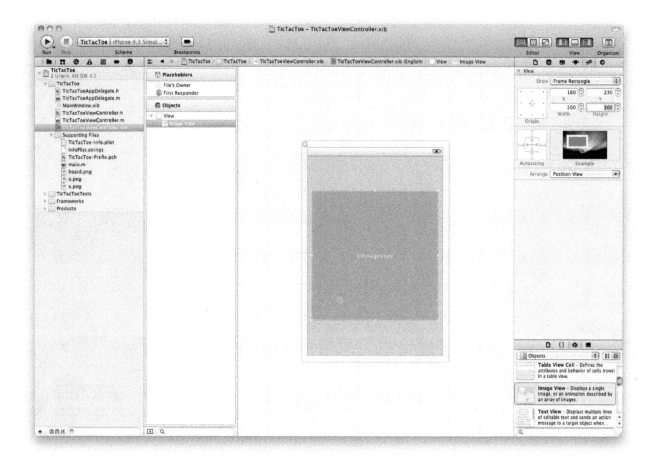

Now, before we add the actual images, let's add all the other views. Drag another image view onto the first one and resize it to 90 by 90 and name it c1.

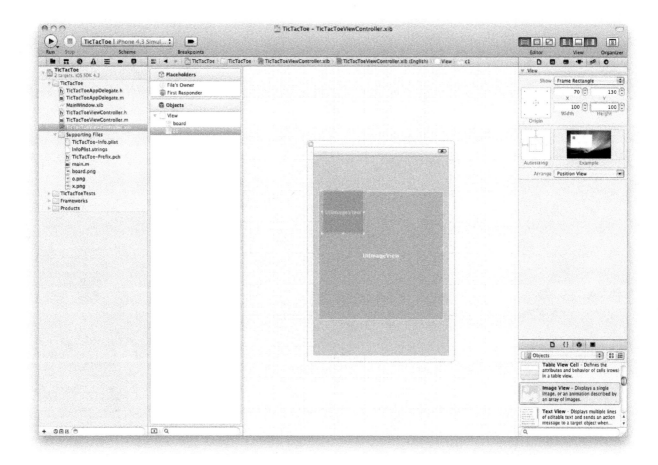

Select c1 and copy it. Paste eight times to make a total nine cells, place them on the board and name them sequentially, c1-c9.

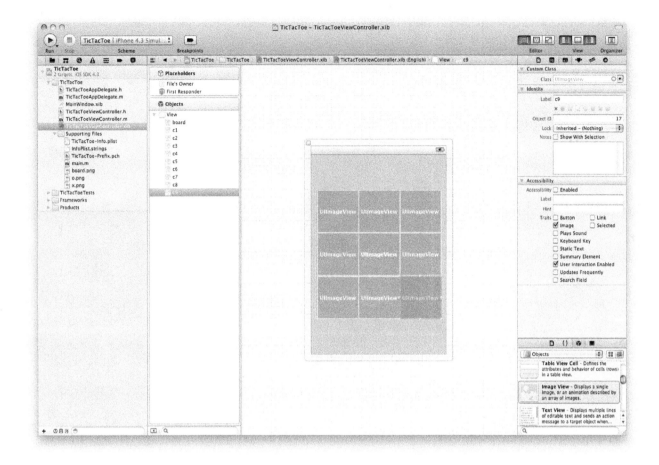

Open the Assistant while in IB to see where it's looking for code – in this case, TicTacToeViewController.h (where these objects should be declared).

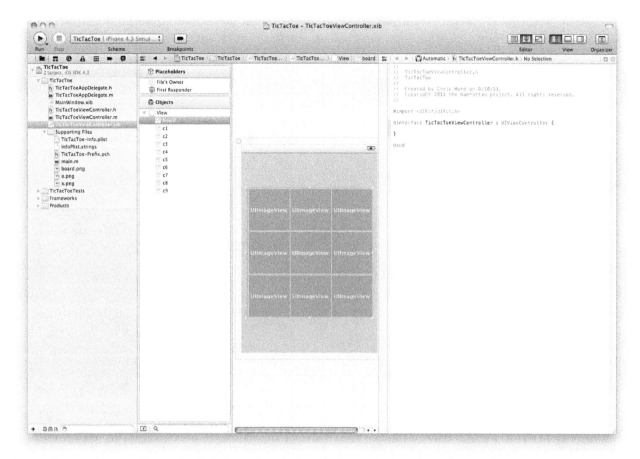

Open the Assistant. Control-click board and drag it from the Dock to the Assistant, where it will declare the object as part of the @interface...

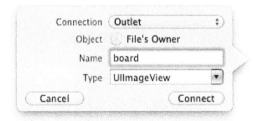

and include a @property declaration as well.

```
#import <UIKit/UIKit.h>

@interface TicTacToeViewController : UIViewController {

    UIImageView *board;
}
@property (nonatomic, retain) IBOutlet UIImageView *board;

@end
```

Using the same method, declare c1 through c9.

```
#import <UIKit/UIKit.h>

@interface TicTacToeViewController : UIViewController {

    UIImageView *board;
    UIImageView *c1;
    UIImageView *c2;
    UIImageView *c3;
    UIImageView *c4;
    UIImageView *c5;
    UIImageView *c6;
    UIImageView *c7;
    UIImageView *c8;
    UIImageView *c9;
}
@property (nonatomic, retain) IBOutlet UIImageView *board;
@property (nonatomic, retain) IBOutlet UIImageView *c1;
@property (nonatomic, retain) IBOutlet UIImageView *c2;
@property (nonatomic, retain) IBOutlet UIImageView *c3;
@property (nonatomic, retain) IBOutlet UIImageView *c4;
@property (nonatomic, retain) IBOutlet UIImageView *c5;
@property (nonatomic, retain) IBOutlet UIImageView *c6;
@property (nonatomic, retain) IBOutlet UIImageView *c7;
@property (nonatomic, retain) IBOutlet UIImageView *c8;
@property (nonatomic, retain) IBOutlet UIImageView *c9;

@end
```

Let's insert the board image now.

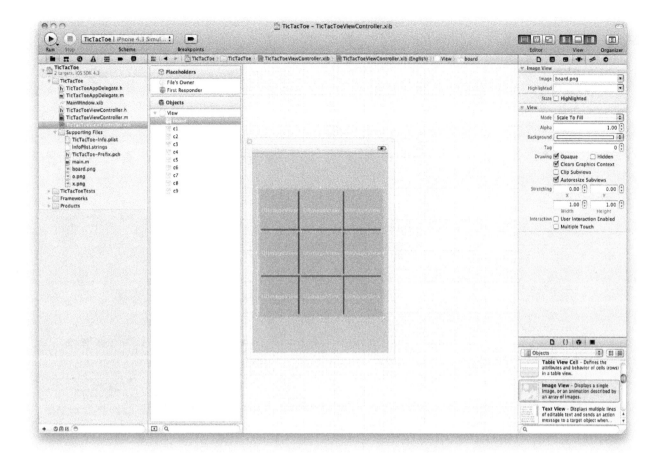

Just use the Attributes Inspector. Go to Image View and use the drop-down menu to select board.png in the Image field.

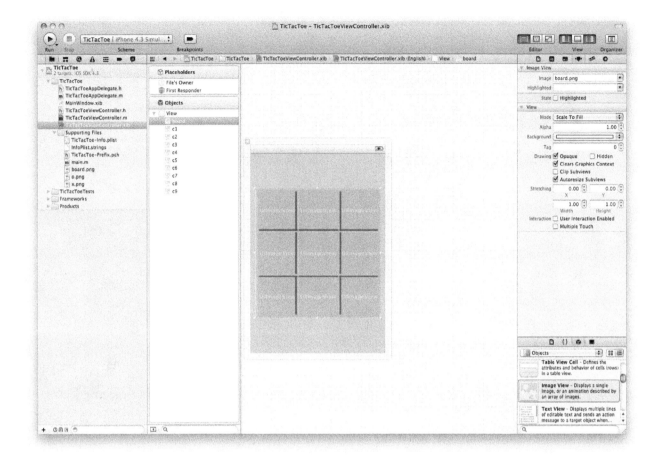

Now, go to the Attribute Inspector and change the Attribute Inspector mode from Scale To Fill, to Center, and you can see the board.

Now, we have a strip across the top and the bottom. We should put a nice label with a name on there for a quality graphic. Maybe a label that says "X goes now..." with a button that says Done. When you hit that button, it says, "O goes now...." When a win condition is reached, it says that either X or O "is the winner!"

The bottom is just a reset button.

Win conditions and reset

So, we've already got nine counters with a state of 0, 1 or 2. We use 1 for X and 2 for O. Logically, we can just check these. Win conditions are 1, 2, 3; 4, 5, 6; 7, 8, 9; 1, 4, 7; 2, 5, 8; 3, 6, 9; 1, 5, 9; and 3, 5, 7. That's eight states. We'll check for a win condition every time the Done button is pressed.

And reset just puts everything back to the start condition and is called when we hit the Reset button. That part's pretty simple. Let's start there.

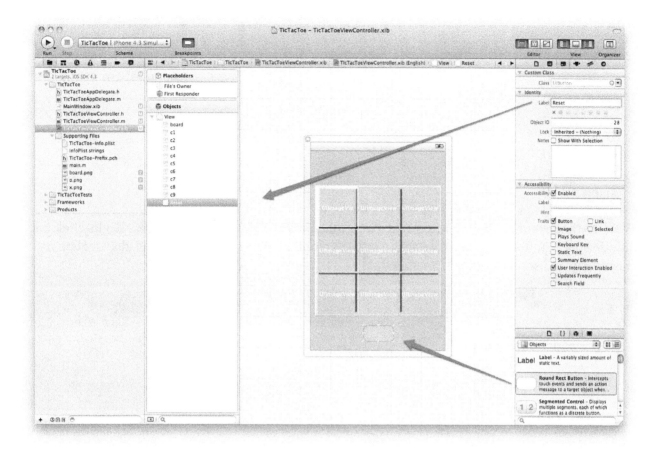

When we highlight the Reset button in the XIB file, the Connection Inspector drops down a list of Sent Events. Right-click and drag from Referencing Outlets to File's Owner. Select the reset method.

Drag from Touches Up Inside to the header, where Xcode will declare an IBAction called reset. Xcode will also set up code for it in the implementation file.

For the reset method, we have to declare it in the header. In the implementation file, we should just be able to use the code from the viewDidLoad method:

```
c1.image = nil;
c2.image = nil;
c3.image = nil;
c4.image = nil;
c5.image = nil;
```

```
c6.image = nil;
c7.image = nil;
c8.image = nil;
c9.image = nil;

counter1 = 0;
counter2 = 0;
counter3 = 0;
counter4 = 0;
counter5 = 0;
counter6 = 0;
counter7 = 0;
counter8 = 0;
counter9 = 0;
```

We'll do the rest of the button setup first. Select the button and click on Assistant. Right-click and drag from the button to the @interface to create an outlet. While we are in there, also declare a @property and set up a - (void)reset method.

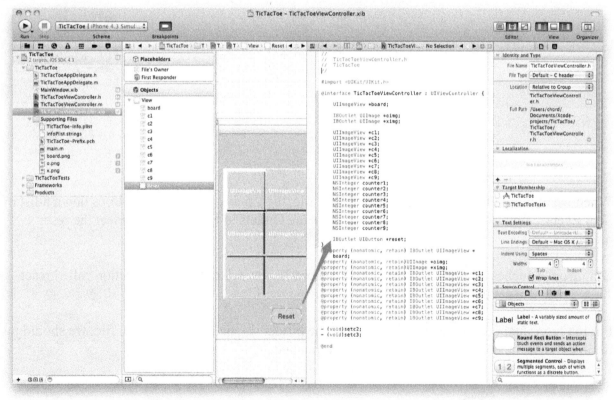

Put a label on there and name it "Tic Tac Toe." Set it up any way you like – we made it red and chose Zapfino 17 point as our font.

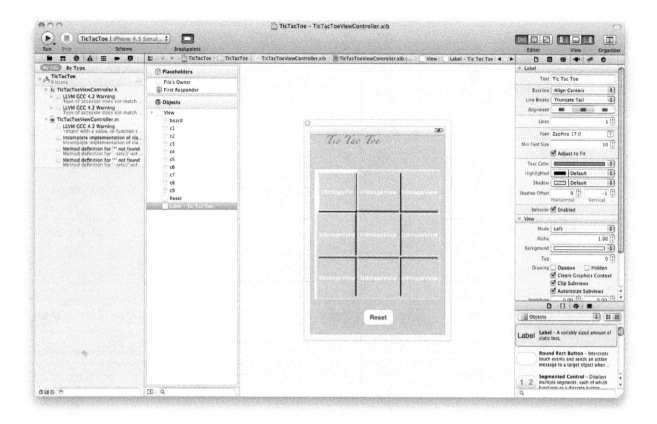

Two items left – another label and a button. Drag them on to the layout. We called the label "X goes now:" and the button "Done." Now we need to hook them up.

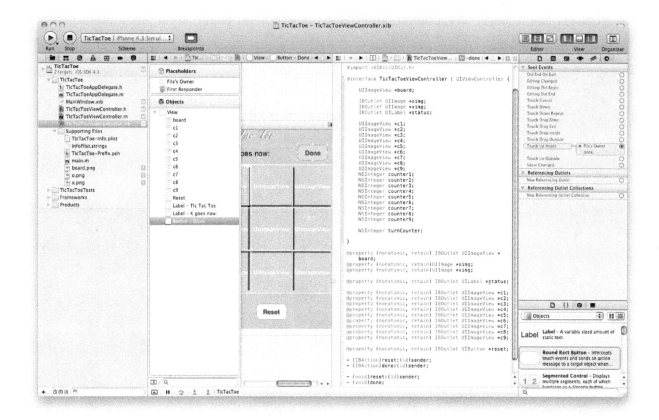

Now, the label needs to be an IBOutlet, so we can change it. Let's do that.

Go to the XIB and select the Done button. Use Assistant to get the header for the view controller. From Connections Inspector, click and drag from Touches Up Inside to the point in the header where the other IBAction is.

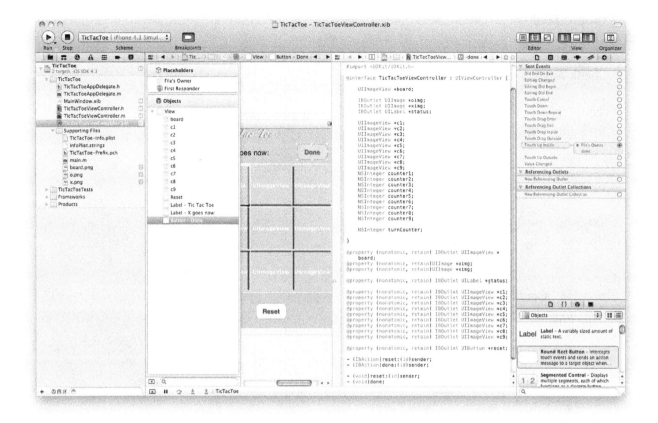

On to the implementation file. We'll need to do the reset method, with the code above. Also, synthesize the button.

Now, to write it. We also created a new NSInteger in the @interface, "NSInteger turnCounter;". To viewDidLoad and reset, we added "turnCounter = 1;".
Now let's make it do something. We're just going to try to send a message that will change the status label.

Add this line in the -done method, "status.text = @"O goes now:";" When the button is clicked, the message changes. Also, add "status.text = @"X goes now:";" to the reset method.

```objc
- (IBAction)done:(id)sender {

    // Updates label to prompt next player
    if (turnCounter == 1) {
        tip = @"O goes now:";
        turnCounter++;
    }

    else {
        tip = @"X goes now:";
```

```
    turnCounter–;
}

// Check for X win conditions

if (counter1 == 1 && counter1 == counter2 && counter2 == counter3) {
    tip = @"X is the winner!";
}
if (counter4 == 1 && counter4 == counter5 && counter5 == counter6) {
    tip = @"X is the winner!";
}
if (counter7 == 1 && counter7 == counter8 && counter8 == counter9) {
    tip = @"X is the winner!";
}
if (counter1 == 1 && counter1 == counter4 && counter4 == counter7) {
    tip = @"X is the winner!";
}
if (counter2 == 1 && counter2 == counter5 && counter5 == counter8) {
    tip = @"X is the winner!";
}
if (counter3 == 1 && counter3 == counter6 && counter6 == counter9) {
    tip = @"X is the winner!";
}
if (counter1 == 1 && counter1 == counter5 && counter5 == counter9) {
    tip = @"X is the winner!";
}
if (counter3 == 1 && counter3 == counter5 && counter5 == counter7) {
    tip = @"X is the winner!";
}


// Some code, revised to check for O win conditions

if (counter1 == 2 && counter1 == counter2 && counter2 == counter3) {
    tip = @"O is the winner!";
}
if (counter4 == 2 && counter4 == counter5 && counter5 == counter6) {
    tip = @"O is the winner!";
}
if (counter7 == 2 && counter7 == counter8 && counter8 == counter9) {
    tip = @"O is the winner!";
}
if (counter1 == 2 && counter1 == counter4 && counter4 == counter7) {
    tip = @"O is the winner!";
```

```
}
if (counter2 == 2 && counter2 == counter5 && counter5 == counter8) {
    tip = @"O is the winner!";
}
if (counter3 == 2 && counter3 == counter6 && counter6 == counter9) {
    tip = @"O is the winner!";
}
if (counter1 == 2 && counter1 == counter5 && counter5 == counter9) {
    tip = @"O is the winner!";
}
if (counter3 == 2 && counter3 == counter5 && counter5 == counter7) {
    tip = @"O is the winner!";
}

    status.text = tip;
}
```

All win conditions defined and operating with no errors.

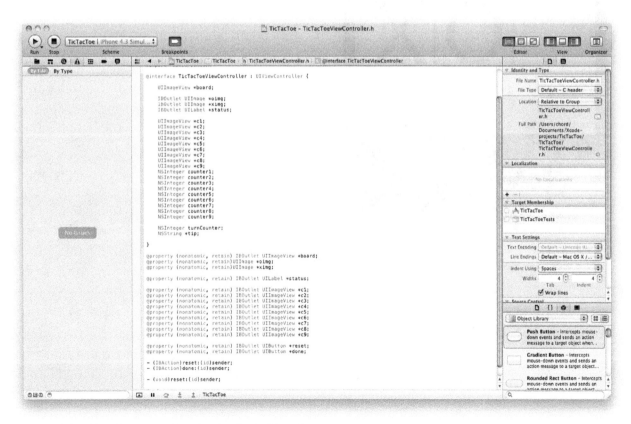

The final application, running in the iOS Simulator.

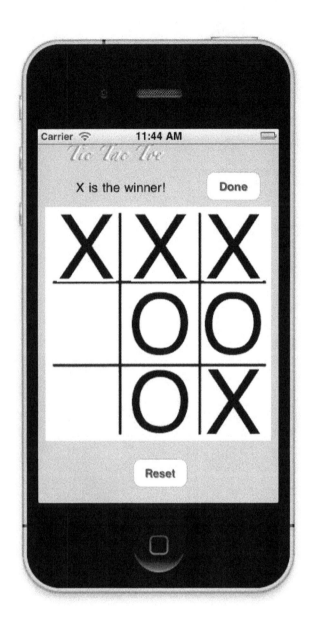

TicTacToeViewController.h

```
//
// TicTacToeViewController.h
// TicTacToe
//

#import <UIKit/UIKit.h>

@interface TicTacToeViewController : UIViewController {

    UIImageView *board;

    IBOutlet UIImage *oimg;
    IBOutlet UIImage *ximg;
    IBOutlet UILabel *status;

    UIImageView *c1;
    UIImageView *c2;
    UIImageView *c3;
    UIImageView *c4;
    UIImageView *c5;
    UIImageView *c6;
    UIImageView *c7;
    UIImageView *c8;
    UIImageView *c9;
    NSInteger counter1;
    NSInteger counter2;
    NSInteger counter3;
    NSInteger counter4;
    NSInteger counter5;
    NSInteger counter6;
    NSInteger counter7;
    NSInteger counter8;
    NSInteger counter9;

    NSInteger turnCounter;
    NSString *tip;

}
```

```objc
@property (nonatomic, retain) IBOutlet UIImageView *board;
@property (nonatomic, retain)UIImage *oimg;
@property (nonatomic, retain)UIImage *ximg;

@property (nonatomic, retain) IBOutlet UILabel *status;

@property (nonatomic, retain) IBOutlet UIImageView *c1;
@property (nonatomic, retain) IBOutlet UIImageView *c2;
@property (nonatomic, retain) IBOutlet UIImageView *c3;
@property (nonatomic, retain) IBOutlet UIImageView *c4;
@property (nonatomic, retain) IBOutlet UIImageView *c5;
@property (nonatomic, retain) IBOutlet UIImageView *c6;
@property (nonatomic, retain) IBOutlet UIImageView *c7;
@property (nonatomic, retain) IBOutlet UIImageView *c8;
@property (nonatomic, retain) IBOutlet UIImageView *c9;

@property (nonatomic, retain) IBOutlet UIButton *reset;
@property (nonatomic, retain) IBOutlet UIButton *done;

- (IBAction)reset:(id)sender;
- (IBAction)done:(id)sender;

- (void)reset:(id)sender;

@end
```

TicTacToeViewController.m

```objc
//
//  TicTacToeViewController.m
//  TicTacToe
//

#import "TicTacToeViewController.h"

@implementation TicTacToeViewController
@synthesize board, oimg, ximg;
@synthesize c1, c2, c3, c4, c5, c6, c7, c8, c9;
@synthesize reset, done, status;

- (void)dealloc
{
    [board release];
    [c1 release];
    [c2 release];
    [c3 release];
    [c4 release];
    [c5 release];
    [c6 release];
    [c7 release];
    [c8 release];
    [c9 release];
    [reset release];

    [status release];

    [tip release];


    [super dealloc];
}

- (void)didReceiveMemoryWarning
{
    // Releases the view if it doesn't have a superview.
    [super didReceiveMemoryWarning];
```

```objc
    // Release any cached data, images, etc. that aren't in use.
}

#pragma mark - View lifecycle


// Implement viewDidLoad to do additional setup after loading the view, typically from a nib.
- (void)viewDidLoad
{
    oimg = [UIImage imageNamed:@"o.png"];
    ximg = [UIImage imageNamed:@"x.png"];
    c1.image = nil;
    c2.image = nil;
    c3.image = nil;
    c4.image = nil;
    c5.image = nil;
    c6.image = nil;
    c7.image = nil;
    c8.image = nil;
    c9.image = nil;

    counter1 = 0;
    counter2 = 0;
    counter3 = 0;
    counter4 = 0;
    counter5 = 0;
    counter6 = 0;
    counter7 = 0;
    counter8 = 0;
    counter9 = 0;

    turnCounter = 1;

    tip = @"X goes now:";
    status.text = @"X goes now:";

    [super viewDidLoad];
}

- (void)touchesBegan:(NSSet *)touches withEvent:(UIEvent *)event {
    UITouch *touch = [[event allTouches]anyObject];


    if (CGRectContainsPoint([c1 frame], [touch locationInView:self.view])) {
```

```
      if (counter1 == 0) {
        c1.image = ximg;
        counter1++;
       }
      else if ( counter1 == 1) {
        c1.image = oimg;
        counter1++;
      }
      else if ( counter1 == 2) {
        c1.image = nil;
        counter1 = 0;
      }
   }

   if (CGRectContainsPoint([c2 frame], [touch locationInView:self.view])) {
      if (counter2 == 0) {
        c2.image = ximg;
        counter2++;
      }
      else if ( counter2 == 1) {
        c2.image = oimg;
        counter2++;
      }
      else if ( counter2 == 2) {
        c2.image = nil;
        counter2 = 0;
      }
   }

   if (CGRectContainsPoint([c3 frame], [touch locationInView:self.view])) {
      if (counter3 == 0) {
        c3.image = ximg;
        counter3++;
      }
      else if ( counter3 == 1) {
        c3.image = oimg;
        counter3++;
      }
      else if ( counter3 == 2) {
        c3.image = nil;
        counter3 = 0;
      }
   }
```

```
if (CGRectContainsPoint([c4 frame], [touch locationInView:self.view])) {
  if (counter4 == 0) {
    c4.image = ximg;
    counter4++;
  }
  else if ( counter4 == 1) {
    c4.image = oimg;
    counter4++;
  }
  else if ( counter4 == 2) {
    c4.image = nil;
    counter4 = 0;
  }
}

if (CGRectContainsPoint([c5 frame], [touch locationInView:self.view])) {
  if (counter5 == 0) {
    c5.image = ximg;
    counter5++;
  }
  else if ( counter5 == 1) {
    c5.image = oimg;
    counter5++;
  }
  else if ( counter5 == 2) {
    c5.image = nil;
    counter5 = 0;
  }
}

if (CGRectContainsPoint([c6 frame], [touch locationInView:self.view])) {
  if (counter6 == 0) {
    c6.image = ximg;
    counter6++;
  }
  else if ( counter6 == 1) {
    c6.image = oimg;
    counter6++;
  }
  else if ( counter6 == 2) {
    c6.image = nil;
    counter6 = 0;
  }
}
```

```
if (CGRectContainsPoint([c7 frame], [touch locationInView:self.view])) {
    if (counter7 == 0) {
        c7.image = ximg;
        counter7++;
    }
    else if ( counter7 == 1) {
        c7.image = oimg;
        counter7++;
    }
    else if ( counter7 == 2) {
        c7.image = nil;
        counter7 = 0;
    }
}

if (CGRectContainsPoint([c8 frame], [touch locationInView:self.view])) {
    if (counter8 == 0) {
        c8.image = ximg;
        counter8++;
    }
    else if ( counter8 == 1) {
        c8.image = oimg;
        counter8++;
    }
    else if ( counter8 == 2) {
        c8.image = nil;
        counter8 = 0;
    }
}

if (CGRectContainsPoint([c9 frame], [touch locationInView:self.view])) {
    if (counter9 == 0) {
        c9.image = ximg;
        counter9++;
    }
    else if ( counter9 == 1) {
        c9.image = oimg;
        counter9++;
    }
    else if ( counter9 == 2) {
        c9.image = nil;
        counter9 = 0;
    }
}
```

```objc
    }
}


- (IBAction)reset:(id)sender {

    c1.image = nil;
    c2.image = nil;
    c3.image = nil;
    c4.image = nil;
    c5.image = nil;
    c6.image = nil;
    c7.image = nil;
    c8.image = nil;
    c9.image = nil;

    counter1 = 0;
    counter2 = 0;
    counter3 = 0;
    counter4 = 0;
    counter5 = 0;
    counter6 = 0;
    counter7 = 0;
    counter8 = 0;
    counter9 = 0;

    turnCounter = 1;

    status.text = @"X goes now:";

}

- (IBAction)done:(id)sender {

    // Updates label to prompt next player
    if (turnCounter == 1) {
        tip = @"O goes now:";
        turnCounter++;
    }

    else {
        tip = @"X goes now:";
```

```
        turnCounter–;
}

// Check for X win conditions

if (counter1 == 1 && counter1 == counter2 && counter2 == counter3) {
    tip = @"X is the winner!";
}
if (counter4 == 1 && counter4 == counter5 && counter5 == counter6) {
    tip = @"X is the winner!";
}
if (counter7 == 1 && counter7 == counter8 && counter8 == counter9) {
    tip = @"X is the winner!";
}
if (counter1 == 1 && counter1 == counter4 && counter4 == counter7) {
    tip = @"X is the winner!";
}
if (counter2 == 1 && counter2 == counter5 && counter5 == counter8) {
    tip = @"X is the winner!";
}
if (counter3 == 1 && counter3 == counter6 && counter6 == counter9) {
    tip = @"X is the winner!";
}
if (counter1 == 1 && counter1 == counter5 && counter5 == counter9) {
    tip = @"X is the winner!";
}
if (counter3 == 1 && counter3 == counter5 && counter5 == counter7) {
    tip = @"X is the winner!";
}


// Sme code, revised to check for O win conditions

if (counter1 == 2 && counter1 == counter2 && counter2 == counter3) {
    tip = @"O is the winner!";
}
if (counter4 == 2 && counter4 == counter5 && counter5 == counter6) {
    tip = @"O is the winner!";
}
if (counter7 == 2 && counter7 == counter8 && counter8 == counter9) {
    tip = @"O is the winner!";
}
if (counter1 == 2 && counter1 == counter4 && counter4 == counter7) {
    tip = @"O is the winner!";
```

```
        }
        if (counter2 == 2 && counter2 == counter5 && counter5 == counter8) {
            tip = @"O is the winner!";
        }
        if (counter3 == 2 && counter3 == counter6 && counter6 == counter9) {
            tip = @"O is the winner!";
        }
        if (counter1 == 2 && counter1 == counter5 && counter5 == counter9) {
            tip = @"O is the winner!";
        }
        if (counter3 == 2 && counter3 == counter5 && counter5 == counter7) {
            tip = @"O is the winner!";
        }

        status.text = tip;

}


- (void)viewDidUnload
{
    //Check vs Pong

    [self setBoard:nil];
    [self setC1:nil];
    [self setC2:nil];
    [self setC3:nil];
    [self setC4:nil];
    [self setC5:nil];
    [self setC6:nil];
    [self setC7:nil];
    [self setC8:nil];
    [self setC9:nil];
    [status release];
    status = nil;
    [super viewDidUnload];
    // Release any retained subviews of the main view.
    // e.g. self.myOutlet = nil;
}

- (BOOL)shouldAutorotateToInterfaceOrientation:(UIInterfaceOrientation)interfaceOrientation
{
    // Return YES for supported orientations
    return (interfaceOrientation == UIInterfaceOrientationPortrait);
```

```
    }
@end
```

Part III: Important iPhone game app programming skills

Debugging your code

Mistakes in your code are known as *bugs*, and bugs can be very frustrating. But it's as simple as this – you're going to make mistakes. You're human; it's only human nature. If you've ever had to type some document that's several pages long, you know that errors will creep in.

When a computer encounters an instruction that it can't understand, it isn't smart enough to make its best guess as to what you want. It stops working and issues a message that has information about why it was confused. This message is called an exception.

Even using the simple examples in this book, there's a chance that things may not have gone as you planned. And that's okay too.

We're going to look at the features that Xcode offers for finding mistakes and correcting them. Sometimes it can even fix the problems for you. The more you learn, the easier it will be to use Xcode's assistance to fix your code.

How to debug and analyze your code

Xcode offers several important pieces of assistance as you're writing your code, to help keep you from making mistakes in the first place. These features are part of Xcode's debugging tools so we'll start with those.

We've already discussed how you can use code completion to see options of commands and variables that might be applicable to your code as you type. Remember the tip we mentioned – if code completion has no information on the code you're trying to type, you could be typing it wrong. You'll also remember that you can see red and yellow exclamation points in the left hand margin of the text editor, and that will be a key indication that there might be trouble with your code. Usually, the red exclamation point indicates the presence of an error that's so severe that your code will not compile or run. Now, however, we're going to talk about some more complex procedures that can help you when your code won't run.

You may have noticed that we have not used one whole portion of Xcode's screen from the diagram we introduced you to in Part I. That is the debugger. If you haven't already done so, open the debugger now. You'll see two panes in the debugger window – the variables pane, on the left, and the console pane, on the right.

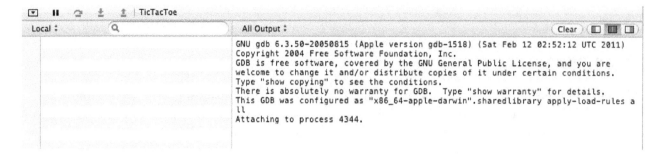

```
GNU gdb 6.3.50-20050815 (Apple version gdb-1518) (Sat Feb 12 02:52:12 UTC 2011)
Copyright 2004 Free Software Foundation, Inc.
GDB is free software, covered by the GNU General Public License, and you are
welcome to change it and/or distribute copies of it under certain conditions.
Type "show copying" to see the conditions.
There is absolutely no warranty for GDB.  Type "show warranty" for details.
This GDB was configured as "x86_64-apple-darwin".sharedlibrary apply-load-rules a
ll
Attaching to process 4344.
```

There are a series of icons in the small toolbar that tops the debugger window. Looking left to right, the icons serve these functions. The downward-pointing arrow closes the window. The "Pause" button stops execution of your code (and turns into a Resume button). The last three icons are to manage functions that are probably new to you, so we'll go into those with more detail. They are, in order, Step over, Step in and Step out.

These buttons are very important because they allow you to resume processing of an application that has been paused, but only by a tiny increment. This is important because, as a programmer, there are many times you will want to change the value of a certain variable. If you do not successfully do this, your program may run, but the results will probably not be what you intended.

Here is how you can use these buttons to help you track the changes that take place in your variables as your program runs. Step over is useful if you only want to examine code in the file you are currently looking at. If it encounters a line that would send it to another part of your program, it "steps over" that line and executes the next line in the current file. If you want to follow the code exactly how it executes at runtime – by following any calls to other files, you can Step in to any file that's included in your project, if necessary. If you do step in to another file and change your mind, you can Step through all those lines of code and return to the next line in your current file.

Controlling debugging with breakpoints

We've said that computer programming comes down to a few basic tasks, and one of those is performing variables while another one is performing operations on those variables. To go back to our Hangman analogy, you'd need to count how many turns the player took, since he or she has a limited amount of guesses. It should be pretty clear that being able to look at the variables as your application runs could be a valuable diagnostic tool. But the Step over, Step in and Step through tools would be very difficult to use if they were not combined with another feature – breakpoints.

Computers are fast. We all know that. If your machine isn't new, or if you have several applications open at the same time, they will sometimes bog down but they process a lot of information quickly. It would be incredibly difficult to stop the processing exactly where you wanted to, to examine the data you wanted to see.

Breakpoints are simply an easy tool to mark stopping points on the project by using the code files that you write. Just click on the margin to the left of any line of your code and Xcode will insert a breakpoint.

Now, when you click Run, Xcode will automatically stop the code at the point you marked. You can see the exact values of your variables, in the variables pane, by clicking the small reveal triangles by every variable name. Additionally, in the console pane on your right, you'll see if there are any messages from the system.

This combination becomes incredibly useful when you have an application that's crashing. If the program is causing serious errors, by inserting breakpoints in your code you can determine what instructions or variables might have created a problem, and see any error messages generated from the crash. When you are through debugging and want your code to run normally, simply click and drag any breakpoint to the left, away from the Editor area. When you release it. It will disappear.

Learning more about the debugger

The debugger is one of the most important tools a software developer will use. We've only talked about a handful of its major functions – ones that beginners will use often. But the debugger is worthy of careful study. As you grow into a more sophisticated programmer, you'll find a variety of tools that will help you make your programs better.

Certainly, you won't want to submit any app to the App Store until you've learned how to check for *memory leaks*. Memory leaks occur when your program reserves memory during its operation, but does not release that memory when it exits. This is a major no-no.

More Objective-C and some alternatives

There are many ways of creating an iPhone app, of course, and Apple does not control all of them. For instance, as long as you are not trying to sell an app on the App Store, anyone with knowledge of web design can create a web app. All you have to do is get your URL to your users, and they can use the built-in browser to access that web site.

Other tools you can use to develop game apps

Unity Technologies offers their powerful Unity game engine for development on iOS. It has been used in more than 1,000 games for the iPhone to this date. Torque, the engine that drives such games as Marble Blast Gold and Minions of Mirth offers a commercial game engine as well.

Additionally, there are open source game engines that you can use for free to help develop your games. These products are usually not as polished, or as user-friendly, as their commercial counterparts. Also, these projects tend to periodically spring up and die out, so we won't even try to list them here. A simple web search will turn up several promising candidates.

Adobe Flex has options that allow users to create mobile apps for the iPhone. Under Apple's current developer's guidelines, this is allowed. This approach may be especially interesting to anyone who has experience developing website animations using Adobe Flash, as there are similarities between the programs.

Other programming languages

Although Objective-C is considered the standard language for developing iPhone apps, if you are familiar with any other programming language, there's a good chance you can bring some of that knowledge into Xcode. Xcode has excellent support for the C and C++ programming languages as well. There are ways to use the C#, Python, Ruby, Perl languages (and more) to handle connections to Apple's interface objects. These methods are not for beginners but it's good to know you can frequently use other technology skills you may have already learned.

Software libraries

We've already talked about the frameworks that Apple provides to assist programmers by providing a ready-made set of code to handle many common programming tasks. Well, there are also plenty of third-party software libraries that offer useful classes and methods for game designers. You can purchase commercial frameworks that will speed your game development skills, but there are free alternatives as well.

One primary framework that is freely available to developers is socos2D (http://www.cocos2d-iphone.org/). This framework can be thought of as a full-fledged game-engine, at least so far as the effects you can achieve. However, it will not offer any special interface to aid in game creation, but the powerful software library has been used by thousands of iPhone developers.

Tools and techniques to improve your apps

Creating animations

There are two main types of animations you will use in creating game apps for the iPhone. Many of the animations that you commonly see in iPhone app navigation are more or less built into the system. The way pages move off the screen as you swipe to a new one is built into the system. The way a page full of listings scroll as you swipe you fingers up or down a table of data (say, your iTunes playlist) – that's built-in too. Later, when you are more advanced, there are easy ways to override some of these behaviors so you can customize them.

There are other kinds of animation, or course. These can be as complex as the sophisticated first-person shooter, or as simple as a picture-puzzle game that relies on art, story or mood as much as gameplay. Fortunately, Apple has already included several pieces of code to perform important, basic animation tasks, like moving objects around the screen.

We'll explore that vital technique in our next tutorial. Now, we're going to make our own adaptation of the classic arcade game Pong. For those of you too young to remember Pong, it is basically a highly simplified version of table tennis produced by game maker Atari in the 1970s. It was the first widely successful commercial arcade game. You can find numerous emulators online as games you can download to a computer, play in your browser, or in a variety of gaming platforms, like the Xbox.

Animating a moving object

There are several libraries of code that can create animations included in the code Apple supplies with Xcode. However, we will use techniques that are available in the iPhone interfaces that we have already used – UIImageView. You'll see how to move these objects, and allow your player to move objects so that they affect each other. This is a fundamental skill you will use in a variety of contexts.

Simple game physics

Another key aspect of creating animations is called "game physics." Now, you don't have to have a physics degree to create these game affects, but the rules of mathematics and of the physical world do apply. In our case, for Pong, we will want to make two paddles and a ball. The ball should bounce off the paddle whenever a paddle comes into contact with it. This is the other major skill you'll learn in this tutorial.

Important details to polish your app

It's easy to add little details to make your app more polished. Add an icon for your app simply by dragging it onto the App Icon spaces in the Summary tab of your project. It needs to be 57 x 57 or 114 x 114 in high definition. You can just drag that into the project too. It needs to be a PNG.

You can also easily add a startup screen by just placing in an image called Default.png into your project. No special code needed. It should be about 320 x 480 pixels.

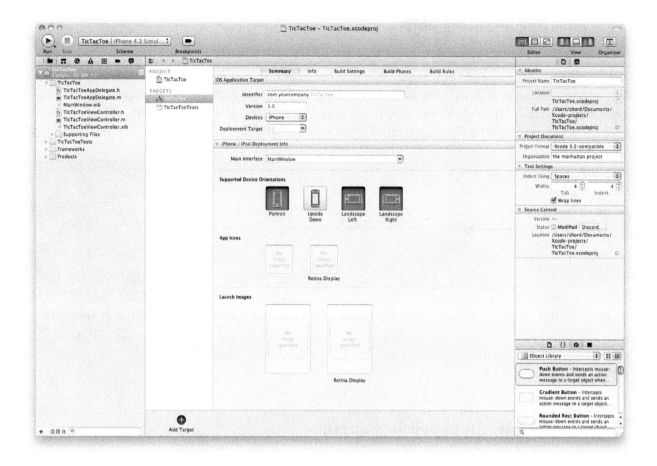

Tutorial 3: Pong

The basic goal of Pong is a simple one. Two players control virtual "paddles" as they knock a virtual "ball" back and forth between them. If the ball hits the sides of the screen, it bounces, and remains in play. If it goes off either end, the opposing player scores a point.

We will begin by placing image views on the screen, as we have done in our previous examples, but this time we will introduce movement to the image views and see how we can make them react.

At the end of this tutorial, you'll see the actual PongViewController files we used to build and run the examples that you see here. They will be especially useful if you are unsure where to put code from this chapter. Just like the Tic Tac Toe tutorial, we urge you to enter the code by hand. It will be quick, using Xcode's code completion feature, and it's important to get a feel for how code completion works. It's also good to see the different colors Xcode uses to color code your syntax, and see where Xcode pops up alerts and warnings.

Getting started

Create a new project called Pong. Choose a View-Based Template. Click Next.

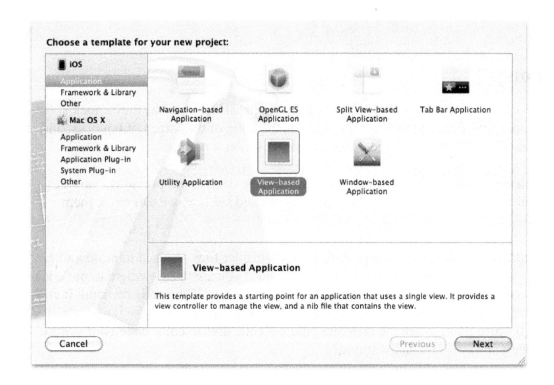

Name it "Pong". Click Next.

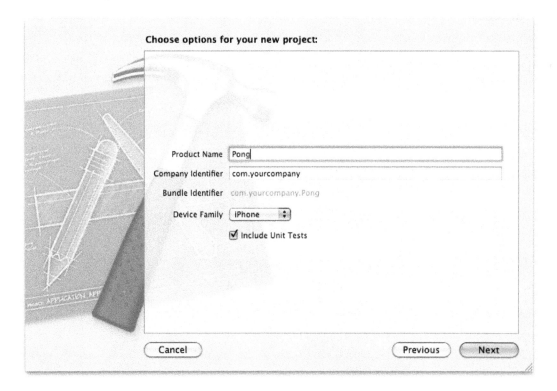

First we need to place some image views. We need a big one to be the court, and two paddles and a ball. Drag one big image view onto the window and let it resize to fill the whole window. Set the background color to black.

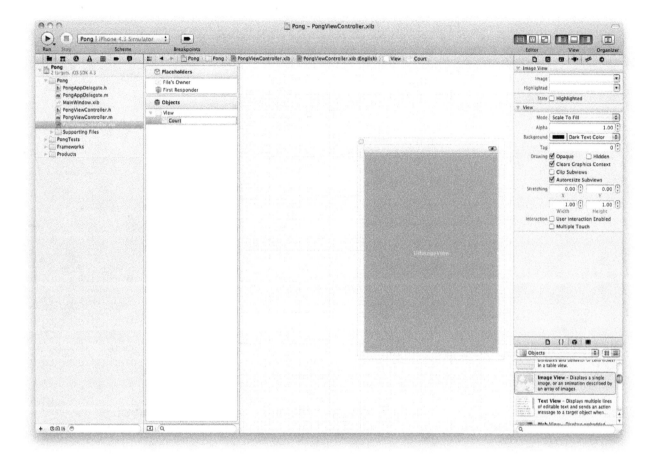

Drag another image view onto the Court. Name it Paddle1. Use the Size tab to make it 75 x 40 pixels. Use the Attributes inspector to set the background color to Green.

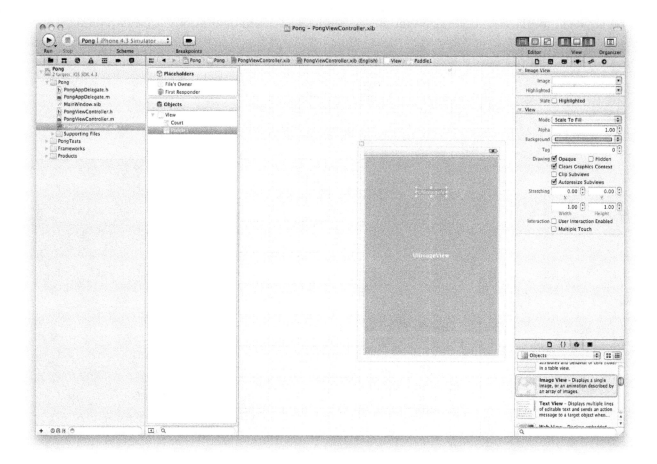

Used Command-D to duplicate it, and change the name of the new copy to Paddle2.

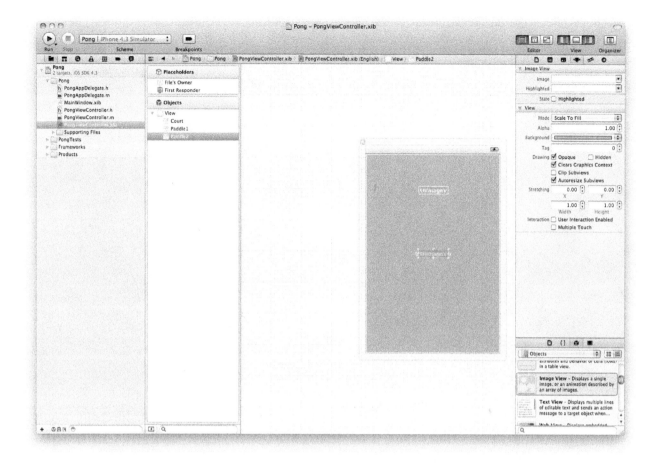

Drag one last image view on there, set the color to Green, size it 16 x 16 and called it Ball.

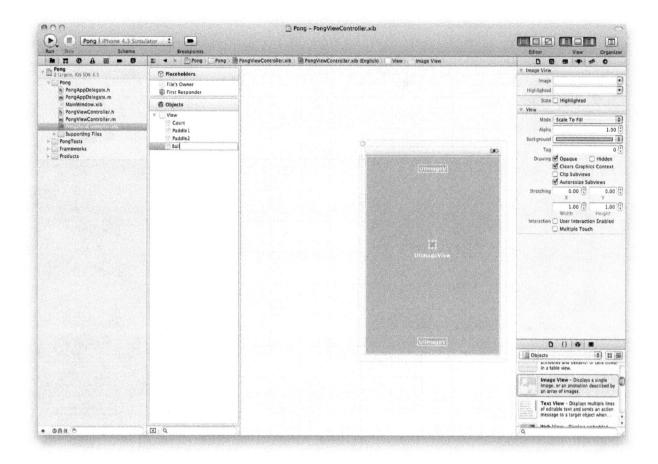

Now, click on the Assistant icon to see the associated code, and declare the IBOutlets by right-clicking on each of the interface objects and dragging them over.

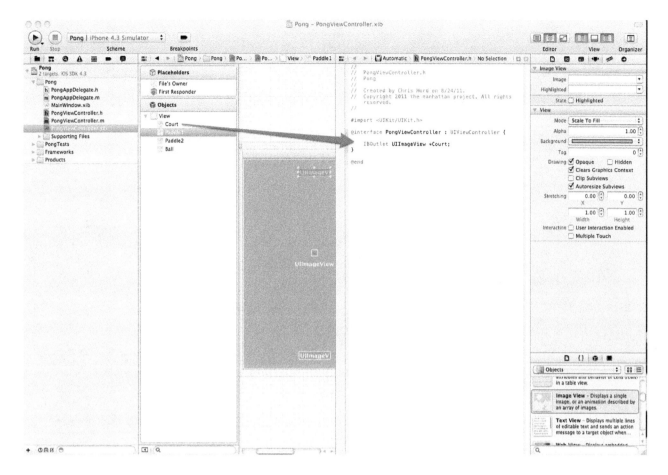

This is what it should look like when you're done.

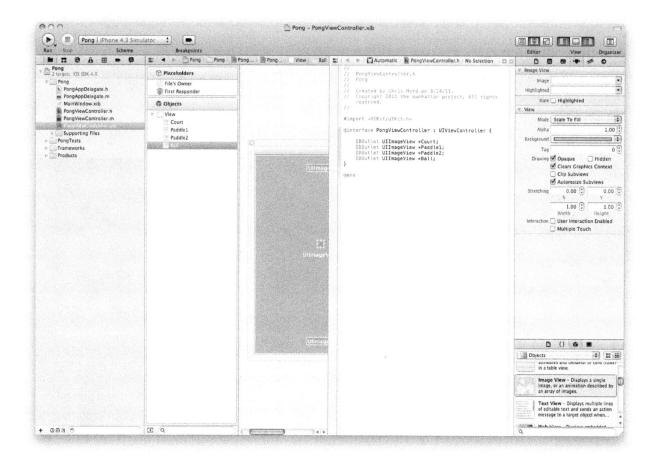

Next, we need to create properties and synthesize these.

Go to PongViewController.h and add the following lines to the file, after the @interface but before @end:

#import <UIKit/UIKit.h>

@interface PongViewController : UIViewController {

   IBOutlet UIImageView *Court;
   IBOutlet UIImageView *Paddle1;
   IBOutlet UIImageView *Paddle2;
   IBOutlet UIImageView *Ball;
}

@property (nonatomic, retain) IBOutlet UIImageView *Court;
@property (nonatomic, retain) IBOutlet UIImageView *Paddle1;
@property (nonatomic, retain) IBOutlet UIImageView *Paddle2;
@property (nonatomic, retain) IBOutlet UIImageView *Ball;

@end

Next, go to PongViewController.m and synthesize the methods. Just add this line after @implementation:

@synthesize Court, Paddle1, Paddle2, Ball;

Now, press run and you should see this!

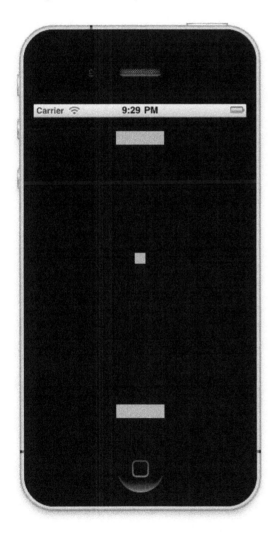

Using the techniques we just discussed, create a center court line by yourself for aesthetics (it doesn't actually do anything). If you get stuck, here are the instructions, but do as much of it as you can. Go to PongViewController.xib. Drag another image view from the Library to the window. Resize it to 320 x 10 and set the background color to Green. Move it to the center of the window, using the guides to help you. Name it Line. Don't forget to declare an IBOutlet in the @interface section of PongViewController.h. In PongViewController.m, you can just add the word "Line" to all the methods we've already synthesized.

Save the project. Run it again and you should get something like this.

 If you didn't, you may need to read the next section on debugging your code. But skim through this section, at least. After all, these are all the steps you're going to have to take when you come back.

After you've had a chance to look at the current state of your app, stop running it. We're going to add logic, to get things moving around here.

MVC and your logic – design patterns turn up again

All this time, we've been talking about the model, the view and the controller. You created the view when you laid your project out in Interface Builder. You hooked that view up to the controller when you declared each interface object in PongViewController.m. Now, you have to think about your logic – the part that tells the controller what to do.

Go to PongViewController.m. You'll notice that certain methods should already be created for you. Here's a quick overview of what we've got:

dealloc – releases all the objects when they are done. You always want to do this, until you are some kind of iPhone guru/expert

didReceiveMemoryWarning – leave this as is. Apple provides a basic method

viewDidLoad – you can use this to do additional setup as your app launches. Leave this for now

viewDidUnload – cleans up additional memory as you release objects. You can leave this as well

shouldAutorotateToInterfaceOrientation – you can change this more easily by selecting your project file in the File Pane, your target "Pong," in the Dock.

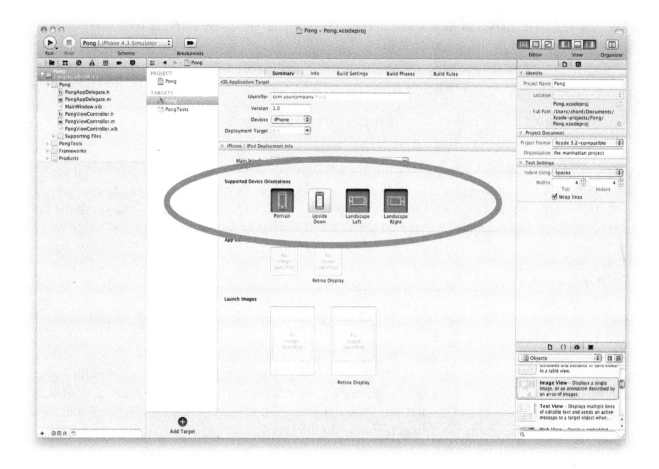

Our final step in this part of the tutorial is to get the ball moving. In fact, we need a game loop that will move the ball. We used this code:

```
-(void) gameLoop {

    Ball.center = CGPointMake(Ball.center.x + BallSpeed.x , Ball.center.y + BallSpeed.y);

    if(Ball.center.x > self.view.bounds.size.width || Ball.center.x < 0) {
        BallSpeed.x = -BallSpeed.x;
    }

    if(Ball.center.y > self.view.bounds.size.height || Ball.center.y < 0) {
        BallSpeed.y = -BallSpeed.y;
    }

    if(CGRectIntersectsRect(Ball.frame,Paddle1.frame)) {
        if(Ball.center.y < Paddle1.center.y) {
            BallSpeed.y = -BallSpeed.y;
        }
```

```
        }

    if(CGRectIntersectsRect(Ball.frame,Paddle2.frame)) {
        if(Ball.center.y > Paddle2.center.y) {
            BallSpeed.y = -BallSpeed.y;
        }
    }

}
```

Let's take a minute to analyze our code. By now, part of this syntax should begin to look familiar to you and, with a little interpretation, you can begin to see the connection between the concepts and the program.

"Ball" is the name we gave to the image view that represents our ball. Center is a property of Ball that tells where the center point of the ball is. CGPointMake is a tool supplied by Apple to conveniently group together the points that make up a geometric shape. There are a variety of handy "CG" tools that will help you move objects, detect collisions and more. The part after the equal sign is more complex. Looking inside the parentheses first, we take the Ball's center and add the variable for BallSpeed.x, moving the center by the value of BallSpeed.x, along the X axis. Then we do the same along the Y axis. Now, the key to remember here is that the gameLoop will continue repeating and, every time it repeats, the ball will move slightly – animating the ball.

Similarly, the rest of the code constantly checks two other ongoing concerns. The first two if statements check to see if the ball reaches the edge of the screen. If so, the ball is reflected back. We do this by checking the location of Ball.center again. The screen is laid out according to *Cartesian coordinates* – a pair of numbers that show where a point would be on a grid.

NOTE: For some reason, Apple's x, y coordinate system is not classic Cartesian. Normally, the numbers to indicate the location of a point start in the lower left-hand corner as 0, 0. The first number, x, increases as the point gets higher and the second, y, increases when the point moves to the right. In Apple's system, x is reversed. So 0, 0 is in the upper left-hand corner and the value of x increases as the point moves downward. Don't be fooled!

The final two if statements handle collisions. We use another "CG"-themed tool, this time, CGRectIntersectsRect. It does exactly what its name implies. You pass it the names and locations of two objects and it will check to see if the objects intersect. Note that, in this instance, we use the "frame" property instead of center. Frame consists of every point around the edge of your object, so it's a perfect tool to check for collisions.

We also added some lines to viewDidLoad to give the ball an initial velocity:

```
BallSpeed = CGPointMake(4, 5);
    [NSTimer scheduledTimerWithTimeInterval:0.01 target:self selector:@selector(gameLoop)
userInfo:nil repeats:YES];
```

...and added BallSpeed to the @synthesize line.

We added "CGPoint BallSpeed;" to the header @interface section and "@property(nonatomic) CGPoint BallSpeed;" to the properties.

To implement paddle movement, we'll need to add the touchesBegan and touchesMoved methods. All touchesBegan does is send a message to touchesMoved:

```
-(void) touchesBegan:(NSSet *)touches withEvent:(UIEvent *)event {

    [self touchesMoved:touches withEvent:event];

}
```

Next, we create touchesMoved. This will see which paddle was touched and move it to follow the user's finger:

```
- (void)touchesMoved:(NSSet *)touches withEvent:(UIEvent *)event {
    UITouch *touch = [[event allTouches]anyObject];
    CGPoint location = [touch locationInView:self.view];

    if (CGRectContainsPoint([Paddle1 frame], [touch locationInView:self.view])) {
        // move the image view
        CGPoint xLocation = CGPointMake(location.x, Paddle1.center.y);
        Paddle1.center = xLocation;

    }

    if (CGRectContainsPoint([Paddle2 frame], [touch locationInView:self.view])) {
        // move the image view
        CGPoint xLocation = CGPointMake(location.x, Paddle2.center.y);
        Paddle2.center = xLocation;
    }
}
```

Adding scoring to you game

In our gameLoop, we already checked to see if the ball hits either end of the screen in our code for determining when the ball bounces. Just use a conditional OR to see if the ball is going out of bounds. It checks self.view.bounds.size.width for the right-hand boundary but only checks against 0 for the left. A similar technique uses height and 0 for the top and bottom. So, you'd use similar code to score. If it goes past height, the player wins the point. If it goes past 0, the other player wins the point.

So, back we go to the XIB file. Drag labels onto the lower left and upper right-hand corners and label them each "0". We set the Font to Courier New, centered the text and changed the Text Color to Green.

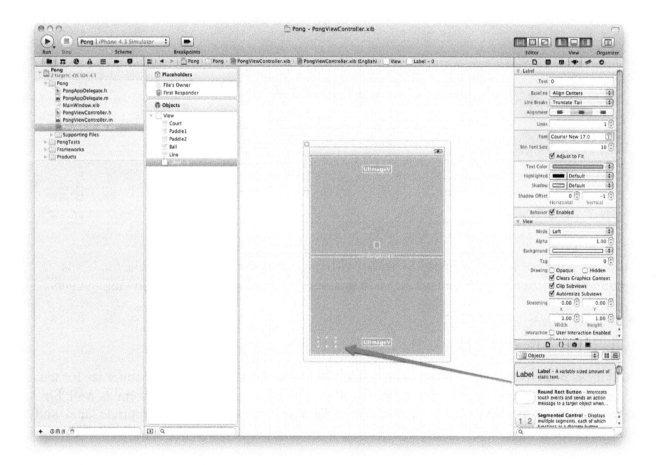

Now we do the same for the upper right.

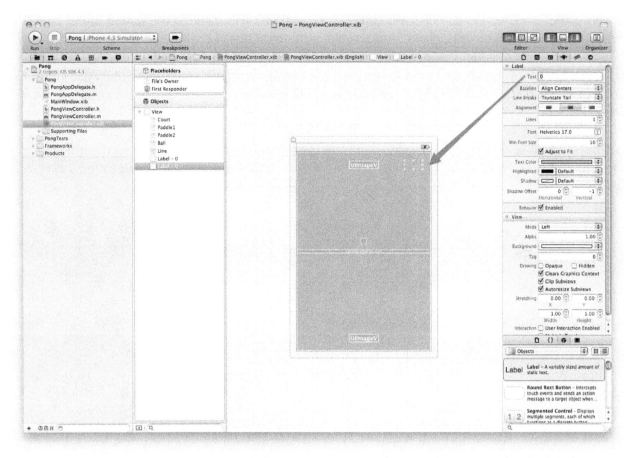

Now, we have our labels. We need to declare two integers. First, we have to make the labels IBOutlets, so we can hook them up. Let's do that now. We'll also create the following integers:

NSInteger player1ScoreNow;
NSInteger player2ScoreNow;

Add those lines to the @interface of you header file. Next, we have to declare properties for the integersdeclared properties for player1Score and player2Score and synthesize them as well. So theoretically, all we need to do is write two lines sending a message to the appropriate label, and then hook these up in IB.

We just added these two lines to our scoring logic, which should do it:

player1Score.text = [NSString stringWithFormat:@"%d",player1ScoreNow];
player2Score.text = [NSString stringWithFormat:@"%d",player2ScoreNow];

Next, let's try hooking them up. Go to PongViewController.xib and click on the score label by paddle1. Go to the Connections Inspector and click on the little circle next to New Referencing Outlet, and drag it to File's Owner.

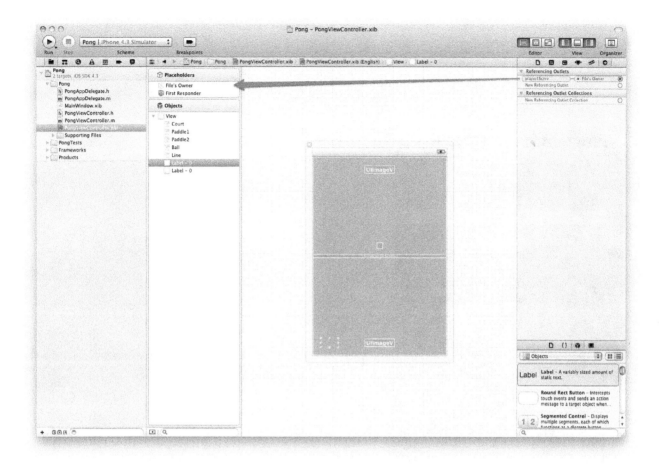

A little box will pop up and you can choose the player1Score method.

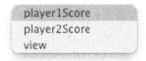

Repeat those steps with the other label and chose player2Score instead. Run it, and you should see scores!

So, scoring becomes this:

```
// Scoring – Uses the same motion logic for the boundaries on either end

if(Ball.center.y > self.view.bounds.size.height) {
    player1ScoreNow++;
}
```

```
if(Ball.center.y <= 0) {
   player2ScoreNow++;
}
```

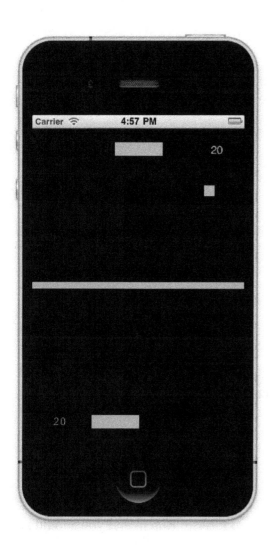

A simple AI

Now, the way we have this game set up, you can play against an opponent, with each of you moving one paddle. However, the iPhone has a small screen and this could get cramped to try to play. So we are going to create our first computer opponent, so a player can play by themselves.

A computer player is sometimes referred to as an *AI*, or *artificial intelligence*. The term is an exaggeration. Game AI usually doesn't have any real intelligence of its own – it just follows a series of rules, covering several situations that might occur. Fortunately, the one for Pong can be very simple. We've already seen how you can use the property "center" to quickly determine the location of an object.

All we want is for our computer paddle to move in the same directions as the ball, to increase the odds of successfully returning the ball. Because the AI will have to constantly check the location of the ball, we'll put this code into the gameLoop. Add this code:

```
// Computer player "AI." You may have to adjust the computer's speed, below.

if(Ball.center.x < Paddle1.center.x) {
    CGPoint destination = CGPointMake(Paddle1.center.x - 1, Paddle1.center.y);
    Paddle1.center = destination;
}

if(Ball.center.x > Paddle1.center.x) {
    CGPoint destination = CGPointMake(Paddle1.center.x + 1, Paddle1.center.y);
    Paddle1.center = destination;
}
```

Create a reset function

Generally, iPhone apps don't exit like applications on a Mac exit. The app essentially stops – right where it is. That's a messy effect for our app. There are many ways to create a reset function – we looked at one way to do it in our Tic Tac Toe tutorial. This time, we'll create a game that resets when it reaches a certain socre.

Go to PngViewController.h and declare gameReset – - (void) gameReset;. In the implementation file, we just add this:

```
- (void) gameReset {

    player1ScoreNow = 0;
    player2ScoreNow = 0;

    player1Score.text = [NSString stringWithFormat:@"%d",player1ScoreNow];
    player2Score.text = [NSString stringWithFormat:@"%d",player2ScoreNow];

}
```

Now, we just need to send a message to cause the reset. Let's add a conditional to gameLoop:

```
// Resets the game when the either player gets a score of 11

if (player1ScoreNow >= 11 || player2ScoreNow >= 11) {
    [self gameReset];
}
```

Make a small icon in Preview, using Tools > Adjust Size.... to make it 57 x 57 pixels and name it PongIcon.png. Default.png should be 320 x 480 pixels. Make a Default.png. Drag it over to the Project Summary window. Accept the dialog.

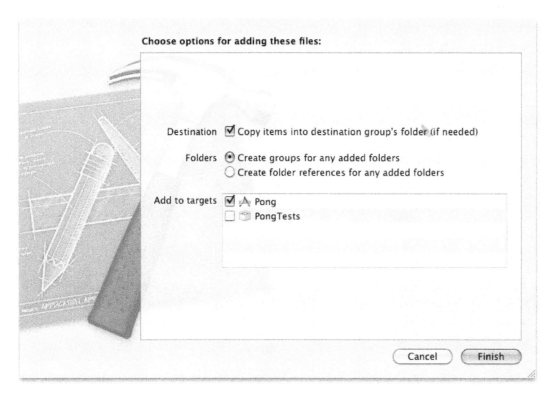

The Icon looks better.

And the game runs.

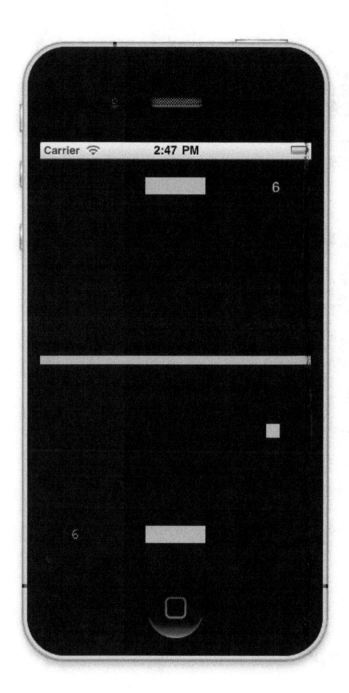

Now, let's remember we need to release all this stuff. We need to release the new labels == player1Score and player2Score. Add these lines to dealloc:

```
[player1Score release];
[player2Score release];
```

Also add this, which is similar to viewDidUnload – which is only there if you get a memory warning.

```
[player1Score release];
player1Score = nil;
[player2Score release];
player2Score = nil;
```

Congratulations! Not only have you animated a moving object, performed collision detection, instituted a basic AI and created pieces that your player can move, you've begun to practice the important task of memory management.

PongViewController.h

```
//
//  PongViewController.h
//  Pong
//

#import <UIKit/UIKit.h>

@interface PongViewController : UIViewController {

    IBOutlet UIImageView *Court;
    IBOutlet UIImageView *Paddle1;
    IBOutlet UIImageView *Paddle2;
    IBOutlet UIImageView *Ball;
    IBOutlet UIImageView *Line;

    IBOutlet UILabel *player1Score;
    IBOutlet UILabel *player2Score;

    NSInteger player1ScoreNow;
        NSInteger player2ScoreNow;

    CGPoint BallSpeed;

}

@property (nonatomic, retain) IBOutlet UIImageView *Court;
@property (nonatomic, retain) IBOutlet UIImageView *Paddle1;
@property (nonatomic, retain) IBOutlet UIImageView *Paddle2;
@property (nonatomic, retain) IBOutlet UIImageView *Ball;
@property (nonatomic, retain) IBOutlet UIImageView *Line;

@property (nonatomic, retain) IBOutlet UILabel *player1Score;
@property (nonatomic, retain) IBOutlet UILabel *player2Score;


@property(nonatomic) CGPoint BallSpeed;

- (void) gameReset;
```

@end

PongViewController.m

```
//
//  PongViewController.m
//  Pong
//

#import "PongViewController.h"

@implementation PongViewController
@synthesize Court, Paddle1, Paddle2, Ball, Line, BallSpeed, player1Score, player2Score;

- (void)dealloc
{
    [Court release];
    [Paddle1 release];
    [Paddle2 release];
    [Ball release];
    [Line release];
    [player1Score release];
    [player2Score release];

    [super dealloc];
}

- (void)didReceiveMemoryWarning
{
    // Releases the view if it doesn't have a superview.
    [super didReceiveMemoryWarning];

    // Release any cached data, images, etc. that aren't in use.
}

#pragma mark - View lifecycle

// Implement viewDidLoad to do additional setup after loading the view, typically from a nib.
- (void)viewDidLoad
{
    BallSpeed = CGPointMake(4, 5);
        [NSTimer scheduledTimerWithTimeInterval:0.01 target:self selector:@selector(gameLoop)
userInfo:nil repeats:YES];
```

```
    [super viewDidLoad];
}

-(void) gameLoop {

    // Moves ball and keeps ball on the court
    // NOTE: In iOS, the coordinate system is "backwards" – 0,0 is the upper, left-hand corner.

    Ball.center = CGPointMake(Ball.center.x + BallSpeed.x , Ball.center.y + BallSpeed.y);

    if(Ball.center.x > self.view.bounds.size.width || Ball.center.x < 0) {
        BallSpeed.x = -BallSpeed.x;
    }

    if(Ball.center.y > self.view.bounds.size.height || Ball.center.y < 0) {
        BallSpeed.y = -BallSpeed.y;
    }

    if(CGRectIntersectsRect(Ball.frame,Paddle1.frame)) {
        if(Ball.center.y < Paddle1.center.y) {
            BallSpeed.y = -BallSpeed.y;
        }
    }

    if(CGRectIntersectsRect(Ball.frame,Paddle2.frame)) {
        if(Ball.center.y > Paddle2.center.y) {
            BallSpeed.y = -BallSpeed.y;
        }
    }

    // Scoring – Uses the same motion logic for the boundaries on either end

    if(Ball.center.y > self.view.bounds.size.height) {
        player1ScoreNow++;
    }

    if(Ball.center.y <= 0) {
        player2ScoreNow++;
    }

    player1Score.text = [NSString stringWithFormat:@"%d",player1ScoreNow];
    player2Score.text = [NSString stringWithFormat:@"%d",player2ScoreNow];
```

```objc
// Resets the game when the either player gets a score of 11

if (player1ScoreNow >= 11 || player2ScoreNow >= 11) {
    [self gameReset];
}

// Computer player "AI." You may have to adjust the computer's speed, below.

if(Ball.center.x < Paddle1.center.x) {
    CGPoint destination = CGPointMake(Paddle1.center.x - 1, Paddle1.center.y);
    Paddle1.center = destination;
}

if(Ball.center.x > Paddle1.center.x) {
    CGPoint destination = CGPointMake(Paddle1.center.x + 1, Paddle1.center.y);
    Paddle1.center = destination;
}
}

- (void) gameReset {

    player1ScoreNow = 0;
    player2ScoreNow = 0;

    player1Score.text = [NSString stringWithFormat:@"%d",player1ScoreNow];
    player2Score.text = [NSString stringWithFormat:@"%d",player2ScoreNow];

}

-(void) touchesBegan:(NSSet *)touches withEvent:(UIEvent *)event {

    [self touchesMoved:touches withEvent:event];

}

- (void)touchesMoved:(NSSet *)touches withEvent:(UIEvent *)event {
    UITouch *touch = [[event allTouches]anyObject];
    CGPoint location = [touch locationInView:self.view];

//   if (CGRectContainsPoint([Paddle1 frame], [touch locationInView:self.view])) {
//       // move the image view
//       CGPoint xLocation = CGPointMake(location.x, Paddle1.center.y);
//       Paddle1.center = xLocation;
//
```

```objc
//    }

    if (CGRectContainsPoint([Paddle2 frame], [touch locationInView:self.view])) {
        // move the image view
        CGPoint xLocation = CGPointMake(location.x, Paddle2.center.y);
        Paddle2.center = xLocation;

    }
}


- (void)viewDidUnload
{
    [Court release];
    Court = nil;
    [Paddle1 release];
    Paddle1 = nil;
    [Paddle2 release];
    Paddle2 = nil;
    [Ball release];
    Ball = nil;
    [Line release];
    Line = nil;
    [player1Score release];
    player1Score = nil;
    [player2Score release];
    player2Score = nil;

    [super viewDidUnload];
    // Release any retained subviews of the main view.
    // e.g. self.myOutlet = nil;
}

- (BOOL)shouldAutorotateToInterfaceOrientation:(UIInterfaceOrientation)interfaceOrientation
{
    // Return YES for supported orientations
    return (interfaceOrientation == UIInterfaceOrientationPortrait);
}

@end
```

Part IV: Where to go from here

Where to go from here

Prepare for a long-term process

If there's anything we would emphasize to a beginning programmer, that advice would be to treat programming as a process. It's a trip, not a destination. The best programmers in the world are constantly embracing new challenges. And the most basic novice can easily find many new skills they can add.

When you have a particular vision of a specific game in mind, it can be frustrating to work on basic tasks when there are so many exciting ideas in your head. Game designing and creation are an art, and many creative geniuses work in the field. But there's a reason they call it software engineering, and that they call a software failure a crash. Think of your software like building an airplane. If the fundamental engineering of your software is not correct, it will crash. Users will be frustrated and disappointed. They'll spread bad word-of-mouth, and they won't come back.

Remember that you will have to consult your reference materials regularly to really know what you are doing. Problem-solving, puzzle-solving and mystery-solving are at the heart of creating software. If you can look at your work as an adventure and a learning experience, you'll find success in the end.

Learning resources

Your main resource is always going to be the software documentation. You can access most of it directly from Xcode – a great deal of it is available at Apple's Developer website too. This material can be kind of dry and technical but – trust us on this – good documentation is your best friend. Part of learning how to be a programmer is actually the simpler task of learning how to read documentation. If you know how a command needs to be written, you can figure out how you need to write your command.

Additionally, there are a variety of online forums where you can search for answers to questions similar to yours. You can generally register and ask questions yourself, but be certain to research your question thoroughly first, and get familiar with the etiquette of that board.

TIP: In addition to studying Objective-C, if you want to become an advanced programmer, you will want to familiarize yourself with the C programming language. There are many powerful tools in C that you can easily access in Objective-C when you are more advanced.

Conclusion

In this book, we have shown you how to create an app and install it on your iPhone (iPad or iPod touch). We have also taught you some of the most important tools in an iPhone developer's skill set – making your screen items respond to the user's touch, and making items on the screen move and interact with each other. We've also seen important skills like determining if a player has won the game and creating a point counter or totaling games won. We've created working versions of Tic Tac Toe and Pong. We've even seen how to create icons and startup screens to make our creations look more professional. Just by using the included code and the tools that are available in Xcode (including the documentation), you can learn how to develop more powerful apps.

But we've sped up that process even more by putting forward some of the most important ideas about programming. You will probably use the object-oriented programming paradigm in every beginning project you write. As we've already seen, Apple uses the MVC, delegation and target-action design patterns extensively and repeatedly. As you learn more about programming, keeping these models in mind will help you understand new information.

You've learned how to use Xcode – probably the single most powerful tool for creating iPhone apps. As we've discussed, there are other tools you can use to develop iPhone apps. There are also other IDEs you can use to write Objective-C. But the vast majority of iPhone apps are created in Xcode. We urge you to explore some of these other options, but familiarize yourself with Xcode first. Although we only touched on some of Xcode's features to help you fix and improve your app after you create it, exploring the tools and features that come bundled with Xcode should become a high priority.

We've only had time to touch on some basic aspects of one of the most important aspects of creating iPhone apps – writing Objective-C code. Objective-C is such a powerful and versatile language that it's easy to write whole books just on that subject. Your highest priority should be to get more familiar with Objective-C. Don't get frustrated. Objective-C can be dense and difficult to understand, but now that you know how to interpret the structure and syntax of a file, and are familiar with methods, classes, variables and commands in Objective-C, it will be easier to puzzle things out. Remember, no one knows the whole Objective-C language – even experts frequently have to look up a keyword, technical term or error message.

Also, you've learned about the machinery to produce your app. If you want to create an iPhone game app, you want people to play it. Bottom line? You're going to want to be in the App Store. There are ways to get around this but beginners should focus on that goal. We've learned how to register as an iOS Developer and provision our own iPhone, iPad or iPod touch to run your own apps. You've run apps on the iOS Simulator. And we've discussed some of the technical and design issues Apple will look at when it reviews your app.

We hope you've had some fun working with this guide. Keep moving forward and you'll be surprised and pleased with how quickly your skills can advance. Good luck!

About Minute Help Press

Minute Help Press is building a library of books for people with only minutes to spare. Follow @minutehelp on Twitter to receive the latest information about free and paid publications from Minute Help Press, or visit minutehelpguides.com.